IN THEIR
OWN WORDS

IN THEIR OWN WORDS

A History of the American Negro

1865-1916

EDITED BY MILTON MELTZER

THOMAS Y. CROWELL COMPANY

NEW YORK

I wish to thank the University of Chicago Press and Benjamin A. Botkin for permission to reprint the material on pages 3-6, 34-35, which first appeared in LAY MY BURDEN DOWN, copyright 1945 by the University of Chicago Press; The Macmillan Company for permission to use the passage on pages 125-126 from THE STORY OF JOHN HOPE by Ridgely Torrence, copyright 1948 by Ridgely Torrence; and Hill and Wang, Inc., for permission to reprint the excerpt on pages 164-171 from THE BIG SEA by Langston Hughes, copyright 1940 by Langston Hughes.

Thanks are also due the following for permission to reproduce the illustrations on the pages indicated (all other illustrations are in the editor's collection):

Atlanta University, page 123; Culver Pictures, Inc., pages 1, 7, 24, 43, 53, 58, 72, 76, 90, 107, 115, 127, 133; Langston Hughes, page 163; Picture Collection of the New York Public Library, page 32; Schomburg Collection of the New York Public Library, pages 17, 39, 102, 112, 154.

I am grateful to Anne Grandinetti for her help in the preparation of the manuscript.

Foreword

The *first volume of* In Their Own Words *tried to help the reader understand the life of the American Negro from the arrival of the first blacks in 1619 to the end of the Civil War. The Negro told his story in his own words, through letters, diaries, speeches, autobiographies, newspapers, pamphlets.*

In this volume, which takes up the story with the end of slavery and comes down to the eve of the First World War, the same kind of direct, personal expression is drawn upon. There is one additional source that proved especially valuable: the testimony given by Negroes when they appeared as witnesses before investigating committees of Congress.

This volume opens with ex-slaves telling how it felt to be free, and what they faced in their new birth as persons, not property. To that badly neglected and often distorted postwar era—Reconstruction—perhaps one half of the book is given. It is an undue proportion measured simply by the span of time it covers, but those brief dozen years have had a profound and lasting effect. The opportunities missed for the healthy growth of American democracy are seen in several of the documents that follow. A third volume will bring the story up to the present.

Introductory passages give the reader background for each of the documents. A few documents are printed in full, but most have been shortened, hopefully without damage to their meaning. Paragraphing and punctuation have been modernized for easier reading. A calendar of Negro history, a reading list, and an index should be of additional use.

Milton Meltzer

Contents

IN THEIR
OWN WORDS

When Lee's army surrendered, American slavery came to an end. By the close of 1865, the Thirteenth Amendment, abolishing slavery, became part of the Constitution. A war that had begun with the limited aim of preserving the Union had been turned into a revolutionary crusade for freedom. It was a glorious victory for the abolitionists, Negro and white. For a generation they had labored together to rouse the country's conscience to the sin of slavery. They had been shunned and stoned, beaten, jailed, lynched. But they had gone on, talking, writing, organizing to overthrow the "peculiar institution." And now, 246 years after the first Negroes had been landed in Virginia, the dream of universal emancipation had come true.

The freedom of four million slaves had been dearly bought. They paid heavily with their own blood, for of the quarter of *a million Negroes who served in the Union forces, thirty-eight thousand lost their lives, a death rate 40 per cent greater than the whites'. If their valor needed more proof, there were twenty Negro soldiers and sailors who earned the Congressional Medal of Honor.*

So they were free at last. But what would freedom be like? How would they live? Where would they work? And what about old master? How would he take the change?

In the recollections of those first freedom days taken down from the lips of ex-slaves many years later, you can see the breaking up of old ways and the forming of new. The first passage is from a woman who had been a slave in Mississippi and Tennessee, the second came from South Carolina, and the third from Georgia.

When freedom come . . .

1865

WHEN FREEDOM COME, folks left home, out in the streets, crying, praying, singing, shouting, yelling, and knocking down everything. Some shot off big guns. Then come the calm. It was sad then. So many folks done dead, things tore up, and nowheres to go and nothing to eat, nothing to do. It got squally. Folks got sick, so hungry. Some folks starved nearly to death. Ma was a cripple woman. Pa couldn't find work for so long when he mustered out.

TOBY AND GOVIE

I worked for Massa 'bout four years after freedom, 'cause he forced me to, said he couldn't 'ford to let me go. His place was near ruint, the fences burnt, and the house would have been, but it was rock. There was a battle fought near his place, and I taken Missy to a hideout in the mountains to where her father was, 'cause there was bullets flying everywhere. When the war was over, Massa come home and says, "You son of a gun, you's supposed to be free, but you ain't, 'cause I ain't gwine give you freedom." So I goes on working for him till I gits the chance to steal a hoss from him. The woman I wanted to marry, Govie, she 'cides to come to Texas with me. Me and Govie, we rides that hoss 'most a hundred miles, then we turned him a-loose and give him a scare back to his house, and come on foot the rest of the way to Texas.

All we had to eat was what we could beg, and sometimes we went three days without a bite to eat. Sometimes we'd pick a few berries. When we got cold we'd crawl in a brushpile and hug up close together to keep warm. Once in a while we'd come to a farmhouse, and the man let us sleep on cottonseed in his barn, but they was far and few between, 'cause they wasn't many houses in the country them days like now.

When we gits to Texas, we gits married, but all they was to our wedding am we just 'grees to live together as man and wife. I settled on some land, and we cut some trees and split them open and stood them on end with the tops together for our house. Then we deadened some trees, and the land was ready to farm. There was some wild cattle and hogs, and that's the way we got our start, caught some of them and tamed them.

I don't know as I 'spected nothing from freedom, but they turned us out like a bunch of stray dogs, no homes, no clothing, no nothing, not 'nough food to last us one meal. After we settles on that place, I never seed man or woman, 'cept Govie, for six years, 'cause it was a long ways to anywhere. All we had to farm with was sharp sticks. We'd stick holes and plant corn, and when it come up we'd punch up the dirt round it. We didn't plant cotton, 'cause we couldn't eat that. I made bows and arrows to kill wild game with, and we never went to a store for nothing. We made our clothes out of animal skins.

I STAYED IN PEONAGE

After Sherman come through Atlanta, he let the slaves go, and when he did, me and some of the other slaves went back to our old masters. Old Man Governor Brown was my boss man. After the war was over, Old Man Gordon took me and some of the others out to Mississippi. I stayed in peonage out there for 'bout forty years. I was located at just 'bout forty miles south of Greenwood, and I worked on the plantations of Old Man Sara Jones and Old Man Gordon.

I couldn't git away 'cause they watched us with guns all the time. When the levee busted, that kinda freed me. Man, they was devils; they wouldn't 'low you to go nowhere—not even to church. You done good to git something to eat. They wouldn't give you no clothes, and if you got wet you just had to lay down in what you got wet in.

And, man, they would whup you in spite of the devil. You had to ask to git water—if you didn't they would stretch you 'cross a barrel and wear you out. If you didn't work in a hurry, they would whup you with a strap that had five-six holes in it. I ain't talking 'bout what I heard—I'm talking 'bout what I done seed.

One time they sent me on Old Man Mack Williams' farm here in Jasper County, Georgia. That man would kill you sure. If that little branch on his plantation could talk it would tell many a tale 'bout folks being knocked in the head. I done seen Mack Williams kill folks, and I done seen him have folks killed. One day he told me that if my wife had been good looking, I never would sleep with her again 'cause he'd kill me and take her and raise childrens offen her. They used to take women away from their husbands, and put with some other man to breed just like they would do cattle. They always kept a man penned up, and they used him like a stud hoss.

When you didn't do right, Old Mack Williams would shoot you or tie a chain round your neck and throw you in the river. He'd git them other niggers to carry them to the river, and if they didn't he'd shoot 'em down. Any time they didn't do what he said, he would shoot 'em down. He'd tell 'em to "Catch that nigger," and they would do it. Then he would tell 'em to put the chain round their neck and throw 'em in the river. I ain't heard this—I done seen it.

From *Lay My Burden Down*, edited by B. A. Botkin,
University of Chicago Press, 1945.

THE RIOT IN NEW ORLEANS—PLATFORM IN MECHANICS' INSTITUTE
AFTER THE RIOT (FROM A CONTEMPORARY SKETCH)

The Union armies had smashed the old order. The slaveholding economy of the South lay in ruins. At the war's close, eleven states were out of the Union. Conquered they were—but not subdued, as one Southerner warned. Now they faced the task of rebuilding their life with the land and the labor they had always relied on.

7

But in what direction would the South move? Would it adopt the conqueror's ideas and institutions? His politics and principles? Or would it hold fast to its own, and try to nourish old roots back into life?

Much depended upon what the North would do. The soldiers in blue returned home to prospering farms, humming factories, and spreading cities, to an economy that had grown incredibly fast and strong under the pressures and opportunities of war. The manufacturers and merchants, bankers and brokers, who held the controls saw limitless horizons for expansion and profits. They wanted to sell their new goods, and sell them anywhere to anybody. As their profits piled up during the war they had begun putting the surplus into western lands, mines, and railroads. Now they looked South, to see how they could "northernize" the stricken land. From its coal and iron, timber and turpentine, plantations and railroads, money could be made. As Yankee businessmen prepared to send their dollars South, they thought about how to reconstruct the region to attain the calm conditions required for investments to prosper.

That term—"Reconstruction"—came into popular use during the Civil War. Then it meant the restoration of state governments in the South that would be loyal to the Union. Historians today, however, give it a broader meaning, to cover all the major changes of the postwar period. A new United States was being born out of the old, and men and parties tried to mold its shape. There were many plans for how to reconstruct the South. Each President, from Lincoln and Johnson to Grant and Hayes, had his ideas, and so did various factions in Congress. Outside Washington other forces were pressing their own policies, from Northern abolitionists at one end to Confederate officials at the other.

Lincoln believed that the seceded states should be speedily restored to the Union under presidential guidance. His first plan for Reconstruction, developed in the middle of the war, excluded all Negroes from voting or holding office.

Only a few days before his death, however, Lincoln had told a friend that "the restoration of the Rebel states to the Union must rest upon the principle of civil and political equality of both races." He believed that the Negroes had "demonstrated in blood their right to the ballot." But a man who had been a slaveholder succeeded him in the presidency. Andrew Johnson granted pardons swiftly to many leaders of the Confederacy and made it clear he would let their states back into the Union on very lenient terms. Federal troops were rapidly withdrawn from the South, with only a handful left behind.

Encouraged to set up their own governments and apply for readmission to the Union, the Southern states framed new constitutions and elected their officials. But nowhere was the ballot offered to the Negro. As in slavery times, Southerners—and many in the North—still believed that Negroes were born inferior, and therefore not only unfit to take part in politics but unable ever to learn how. Only the white race—the superior race—could vote, and in the fall elections of 1865 prominent Confederates were put in office everywhere and the great task of Reconstruction placed in their hands. The sign of how they planned to carry it out was visible at once. "Black codes" were adopted by the state legislatures which in all but name restored the Negro to his old position of slave. This is a "white man's government," said the new governor of South Carolina, "and *intended for white men only." To which all the other new governments said Amen.*

If this was what "home rule" meant, the North would not tolerate it. Republican politicians knew that riveting the chains back on the Negro would make the Democratic Party dominant again. Businessmen did not care to put money into a slave economy. And abolitionists were enraged by the attempt to make a mockery of an emancipation bought by four terrible years of war.

In one state after another Negroes held rallies and conventions to protest these bitter fruits of Reconstruction Southern-style. They demanded that oppressive laws be wiped off the statute books and that all political and legal barriers based upon color be torn down. They wanted the right to vote and federal protection from the bands of white hoodlums trying to terrorize the Negro.

Under the Republican leadership of Thaddeus Stevens and Charles Sumner, Congress refused to seat the new Southern congressmen and rejected the President's Reconstruction program. It set up a Joint Committee of Fifteen to get the facts on what was going on in the South and to work out a better Reconstruction plan. The Committee's proposals included a Freedmen's Bureau and a Civil Rights Bill, both of which Congress passed over Johnson's veto, and the Fourteenth Amendment to the Constitution. It declared Negroes were citizens of the United States and entitled to equal treatment before the law. If any state denied or abridged the franchise on account of race or color, that state would lose representation in Congress proportionately.

To get back into the Union, Southern states were asked to

ratify the Amendment. Although the Amendment did not make a direct grant of Negro suffrage, every state but Tennessee at once rejected it.

If further evidence were needed of how the South felt, two spectacular anti-Negro riots broke out that year. In May of 1866, after some dispute between Negro soldiers and the white police force of Memphis, a mob joined the police in a drunken assault upon the city's Negro population that was put down by federal troops only after three days of burning, raping, and pillaging. The toll showed forty-six Negroes killed and over eighty wounded; one white man was injured.

Violence against the Negro continued into the summer. On July 30, a riot erupted in New Orleans when a white mob containing many policemen and ex-Confederate soldiers attacked a Negro-white convention called to consider a Negro suffrage amendment to Louisiana's constitution. Some thirty-four Negroes and four of their white allies were killed and more than two hundred injured.

This was no riot, said General Sheridan, "but an absolute massacre by the police." Congress sent investigators to both Memphis and New Orleans. From the testimony of the ex-slave Sarah Song and J. B. Jourdain come the following two excerpts:

From Memphis to New Orleans . . .

1866

SARAH SONG

Q. Were you in Memphis at the time of the riots?

A. Yes, sir; I was.

Q. What did you see of the rioting?

A. I saw them kill my husband; it was on Tuesday night, between ten and eleven o'clock.

Q. Who shot him?

A. I do not know. There were between twenty and thirty men who came to the house. When they first came, they hallo'd to us to open the doors. My husband was sick in bed and could not get up; he had been sick in bed two weeks—he had the jaundice. I lay there, I was so scared; we have two children who were with us. They broke the outside doors open. I staid in bed till they came in. The inside door was open. They came into the room and asked if we had any pistols or shot guns in the house. My husband said he had one, but it was only a rusty pistol that his little boy had found—it was fit for nothing but the child to play with. Then they told my husband to get up and get it; he got up and gave it to them. I then lighted a lamp after they got the pistol. They told my husband to get up and come out, that they were going to shoot him. They made him get up and go out of doors and told him if he had anything to say to say it quick, for they were going to kill him. If he said anything, I did not hear it.

He stood outside, perhaps a quarter of an hour. They asked him if he had been a soldier; he said he never had been. One of them said, "You are a damned liar; you have been in the government service for the last twelve or fourteen months." "Yes," said he, "I have been in the government service, but not as a soldier." Then another said, "Why did you not tell us that at first?" Then one stepped back and shot him as quick as he said that; he was not a yard from him; he put the pistol to his head and shot him three times. This was between ten and eleven o'clock. When my husband fell he scuffled about a little, and looked as if he tried to get back into the house. Then they told him if he did not make haste and die, they would shoot him again. Then one of them kicked him, and another shot him again when he was down; they shot him through the head every time, as far as I could see. He never spoke after he fell. They then went running right off and did not come back again. . . .

From "Memphis Riots and Massacres,"
Report No. 101, House of Representatives,
39th Congress, 1st Session (Serial No. 1274).

J. B. JOURDAIN

Q. What is your age?

A. I am thirty-four.

Q. How long have you lived in New Orleans?

A. I was born here.

Q. Were you in this city on the thirtieth of July last?

A. Yes, sir; I was here the whole month of July.

Q. Were you in the Mechanics' Institute on that day?

A. Yes, sir; I was there about 12 o'clock. My attention was called to something going on outside; I heard a drum beating as if the military were coming, and I was much satisfied that it was so. As I looked up the street to where I heard the drum, I saw the United States flag flying, and I recognized a procession of colored persons with the flag. Then I went towards them, and as I got to the corner of Canal and Dryades the procession was coming up Dryades Street from below.

When the tail part of the procession, which consisted of boys, came up, there was a pistol fired from a man who was standing on the corner of the banquette [sidewalk]; it was fired by an officer with whom I am well acquainted . . . he was detailed by the police. He fired at the procession—at those colored boys; when he shot, the boys wheeled around. There were two or three shots fired by the same person; I believe it was by the same person. Then the police from the other side rushed and arrested one of these boys, and jerked him and took him to the calaboose. The drum had kept on with the flag, and the boys all ran.

I stood at the corner and did not go any further; I thought I would not go back to the Mechanics' Institute, and I remained there for perhaps ten minutes. On the corner where I was standing I saw the police from Dauphin Street turning up Canal Street, and running with pistols in their hands. I got on the side of the banquette and let them go by. As they passed Dryades Street they were firing in the street there, and the loafers that were there were throwing bricks at the Negroes, and the Negroes, too, were throwing bricks, and as the people came up they commenced firing. They fired to scare the people, but they fired with bullets. After firing some time the street got a little clear, so that they could go in. I followed them. When they got to the Mechanics' Institute they found the door fastened and they could not get in; then they backed out and fired several times through the windows.

Q. Were the windows up or down?

A. They were shut—some of them might have been open—and as they fired they broke the glass. Then the fire bells began to ring and the firemen began to come. The policemen then succeeded in bursting open the doors and went inside. What they did inside I do not know, but in about a quarter of an hour after there were a good many came out wounded, cut up, shot in the face and head, and there were police taking them to the calaboose. As they passed with them the crowd would knock them down and kill them, and some of the police were helping them kill them on the street.

I spoke to the lieutenant of police, with whom I am acquainted—I am acquainted with them all somewhat—and I begged him "For God's sake, stop your men from killing these men so." He gave me no answer, but walked away to the Mechanics' Institute. After a while I spoke to him again; said I, "For God's sake, stop these men from this; I could arrest them all myself." His reply was, "Yes, God damn them; I'll set fire to the building and burn them all." I said no more, but went away. Afterwards I saw a man come out. He was led by a man at each arm; he had no hat on, and his face was all covered with blood. I was looking straight at him, and I said, "That's somebody I know"—I was speaking to myself. When he appeared the crowd cried out, "Kill him." "Kill the damned son of a bitch." I saw it was Dr. Dostie. The officers had him, and were taking him towards Canal Street. The shots were fired while the police had hold of him, and some of the police were wounded by their own men. It was a volley of shots; I saw he dropped, he must have been more than half dead. I remarked, "There is one more." They then rushed back to the Mechanics' Institute, and every man that came out of the Institute was shot or knocked down with a loaded pistol, and when he was down they would shoot him.

From "New Orleans Riots," Report No. 16,
House of Representatives, 39th Congress, 2nd Session (Serial No. 1304).

HENRY MACNEAL TURNER

*A*ngered by the violence in the South, Northerners voted more Stevens-Sumner Republicans into Congress in the fall elections of 1866. As soon as Congress met, it gave the right to vote to Negroes in the District of Columbia. In March, again over Johnson's veto, it launched its own program (called Radical Reconstruction) by dividing the South into five districts under military command, ordering elections for constitutional conventions, and giving Negroes the right to vote.

Beginning that fall, the Southern states, under the eye of the military, held conventions to write the new constitutions the Reconstruction Acts called for. About a million Negroes were now enfranchised, and nearly the same number of whites. Most of the Negroes, long forbidden education whether slave or free,

17

were illiterate, as were about a third of the whites. When regis-
tration was ended, 660,000 whites had qualified to vote, and
700,000 Negroes.

Illiterate though most of the Negroes were, they were no
worse qualified to vote than the immigrants now being herded
to the polls in the thousands by the political bosses of Northern
cities. Given time, they would learn to read and write. Only
two years out of bondage, they had the courage to risk the
vengeance of former masters and to stand up for their rights
as free citizens. Frederick Douglass, granting all that was be-
ing said of the freedman's ignorance, pointed out that "if the
Negro knows enough to fight for his country, he knows enough
to vote; if he knows enough to pay taxes for the support of the
government, he knows enough to vote."

Even after centuries of oppression, leaders could and did
arise. They came from the plantations and the towns to take
their seats in constitutional conventions and in state legisla-
tures, seats that had always been reserved for white planters.
A few had the benefit of formal training; others were almost
wholly self-educated. Many were preachers, some teachers, a
few lawyers, the others farmers or artisans. Fears of the white
South that Negroes, once in office, would seek bloody revenge
proved groundless. Over the South Carolina convention, the
first assembly with a majority of Negro delegates, rippled a
banner with the slogan, "United we stand, divided we fall."

Among the new leaders of the Negro people was Henry
MacNeal Turner. Born free in South Carolina, on his father's
death he had been bound out to a planter and had lived his
young years in conditions little different from slavery. By the
age of twelve he had shown his fearlessness in refusing to per-

mit overseers to beat him. At fifteen he ran away. He learned his ABC's from friendly whites but when others interfered, he taught himself to read and write out of Bible and hymnbook. As messenger in a lawyer's office and then handyman in a Baltimore medical school, he devoured every book and magazine at hand to learn all he could of law, medicine, and theology. When the Civil War came he was the first Negro to be commissioned an army chaplain, serving with a Negro regiment. Turner was elected to the first Reconstruction legislature of Georgia. While he tried to secure better wages for Negro workers, he also moved to assist the whites' economic recovery. But the legislature was dominated by a white majority and in September, 1868, it expelled all its members who were colored. Here is Representative Turner's defense of the Negro's right to hold office, made on September 3.

I shall not beg for my rights . . .

1868

BEFORE PROCEEDING to argue this question upon its intrinsic merits, I wish the members of this House to understand the position that I take. I hold that I am a member of this body. Therefore, sir, I shall neither fawn or cringe before any party, nor stoop to beg them for my rights. Some of my colored fellow members, in the course of their remarks, took occasion to appeal to the sympathies of members on the opposite side, and to eulogize their character for magnanimity. It reminds me very much, sir, of slaves begging under the lash. I am here to demand my rights. . . .

The scene presented in this House, to-day, is one unparalleled in the history of the world. . . . Never has a man been arraigned before a body clothed with legislative, judicial or executive functions, charged with the offense of being of a darker hue than his fellowmen . . . charged with an offense committed by the God of Heaven Himself. Cases may be found where men have been deprived of their rights for crimes and misdemeanors; but it has remained for the State of Georgia, in the very heart of the nineteenth century, to call a man before the bar, and there charge him with an act for which he is no more responsible than for the head which he carries upon his shoulders. . . .

Whose Legislature is this? Is it a white man's Legislature, or is it a black man's Legislature? Who voted for a Constitutional Convention, in obedience to the mandate of the Congress of the United States? Who first rallied around the standard of Reconstruction? Who set the ball of loyalty rolling in the State of Georgia? And whose voice was heard on the hills and in the valleys of his State? It was the voice of the brawny-armed Negro, with the few humanitarian-hearted white men who came to our assistance. I claim the honor, sir, of having been the instrument of convincing hundreds—yea, thousands —of white men, that to reconstruct under the measures of the United States Congress was the safest and the best course for the interest of the State.

Let us look at some facts in connection with this matter. Did half the white men of Georgia vote for this Legislature? Did not the great bulk of them fight, with all their strength, the Constitution under which we are acting? And did they not fight against the organization of this Legislature? And further, sir, did they not vote against it? Yes, sir! And there are persons in this Legislature to-day, who are ready to spit their poison in my face, while they themselves opposed, with all their power, the ratification of this Constitution. They question my right to a seat in this body, to represent the people whose legal votes elected me. . . . We are told that if black men want to speak, they must speak through white trumpets; if black men want their sentiments expressed, they must be adulterated and sent through white messengers, who will quibble, and equivocate, and evade, as rapidly as the pendulum of a clock. If this be not done, then the black men have committed an outrage, and their Representatives must be denied the right to represent their constituents.

The great question, sir, is this: Am I a man? If I am such, I claim the rights of a man. Am I not a man because I happen to be of a darker hue than honorable gentlemen around me?

We have pioneered civilization here; we have built up your country; we have worked in your fields, and garnered your harvests, for two hundred and fifty years! And what do we ask of you in return? Do we ask you for compensation for the sweat our fathers bore for you—for the tears you have caused, and the hearts you have broken, and the lives you have curtailed, and the blood you have spilled? Do we ask retaliation? We ask it not. We are willing to let the dead past bury its dead; but we ask you now for our rights.

You have all the elements of superiority upon your side; you have our money and your own; you have our education and your own; and you have your land and our own, too. We, who number hundreds of thousands in Georgia, including our wives and families, with not a foot of land to call our own— strangers in the land of our birth; without money, without education, without aid, without a roof to cover us while we live, nor sufficient clay to cover us when we die! . . .

You may expel us, gentlemen, but I firmly believe that you will someday repent it. The black man cannot protect a country, if the country doesn't protect him; and if, tomorrow, a war should arise, I would not raise a musket to defend a country where my manhood is denied. The fashionable way in Georgia when hard work is to be done, is, for the white man to sit at his ease, while the black man does the work; but, sir, I will say this much to the colored men of Georgia, as if I should be killed in this campaign, I may have no opportunity of telling them at any other time: Never lift a finger nor raise a hand in defense of Georgia, unless Georgia acknowledges that you are men, and invests you with the rights pertaining to manhood. . . .

From "Participation of Negroes in the Government 1867-1870,"
by Ethel M. Christler, unpublished master's thesis,
Atlanta University, 1932.

PRINTING SHOP AT TUSKEGEE INSTITUTE, WHERE
YOUNG NEGROES LEARNED THE CRAFT

I*t was a great thing to be free,
but it was terribly hard to make your own way in the world,
without money, without land, without friends. It was "root,
hog, or die" in the beginning. Now the four million Negroes
released from slavery were thrown on the job market to com-
pete with white labor. It was a situation made for trouble.
Some white planters, embittered by the loss of their human
chattels, drove the ex-slaves off the plantations. Others, eager
to get labor at the lowest possible cost, were enraged by freedmen who asserted their right to refuse work if they didn't like
the pay. Aiming at this, black codes permitted Negroes to be
sold into temporary bondage for "vagrancy."*

Many Negroes had had enough of plantation life under any terms. To them it would always be tainted with memories of slavery. They moved into the cities, going North as well as South. Others, skilled as blacksmiths, cabinetmakers, bricklayers, tried to find work in their craft or trade but met iron resistance from white artisans who feared their competition. Some employers did not draw the color line, however, especially if it helped them to undermine white unions. Northerners looked South for cheap labor and imported Negroes to beat down a higher standard of living or to break unions. The exploitation of the Negro for such purposes only sharpened the cleavage between Negro and white workers. Very few unions welcomed Negroes into their ranks.

In Rochester, New York, Frederick Douglass, the foremost leader of his people for a generation, saw his own son jim-crowed by a union. In 1869 he made these remarks about it in a speech.

His crime was his color . . .
1869

DOUGLASS [his son Lewis] is made a transgressor for working at a low rate of wages by the very men who prevented his getting a high rate. He is denounced for not being a member of a Printers' Union by the very men who would not permit him to join such Union. He is not condemned because he is not a good printer, but because he did not become such in a regular way, that regular way being closed against him by the men now opposing him.

Suppose it were true that this young man had worked for lower wages than white printers receive, can any printer be fool enough to believe that he did so from choice? What mechanic will ever work for low wages when he can possibly obtain higher? Had he been a white young man, with his education and ability, he could easily have obtained employment, and could have found it on the terms demanded by the Printers' Union.

There is no disguising the fact—his crime was his color.

It was his color in Denver, it was his color in Rochester, and it is his color in Washington to-day. In connection with this subject I have now a word to say of the goodly city in which I have lived for the last twenty years, and where I still reside, a city than which not one in the country is more civilized, refined and cultivated. It abounds in both educational and religious institutions, and its people are generally as liberal and friendly to the colored race as any other in this State, and far more so than most cities outside of the State. Here the common schools have been open to all classes alike for a dozen years, and colored and white children have sat on the same benches, and played in the same school-yards, and at the same sports and games, and they have done so in peace. I can say many good things of Rochester. The Fugitive-Slave bill never took a slave out of its limits, though several attempts were made to do so. When colored people were mobbed and hunted like wild beasts in other cities, and public fury was fanned against them by a malignant pro-slavery press, the colored man was always safe and well protected in Rochester.

And yet I have something against it. One of the saddest spectacles that ever assailed my eyes or pained my heart was presented in that city, and you will pardon me for making mention of it, though it is clearly personal. The same young man who is now at work at the Government printing office in Washington and against whose employment so much feeling has been shown, was the subject. He had just returned from the war; had stood on the walls of Fort Wagner with Colonel Shaw; had borne himself like a man on the perilous edge of battle, and now that the war was nearly over, he had returned to Rochester, somewhat broken in health, but still able and willing to work at his trade. But alas! he begged in vain of his fellow-worms to give him leave to toil. Day after day, week after week, and month after month he sought work, found none, and came home sad and dejected.

I had felt the iron of Negro hate before, but the case of this young man gave it a deeper entrance into my soul than ever before. For sixteen years I had printed a public journal in Rochester; I had employed white men and white apprentices during all this time; had paid out, in various ways, to white men in that city little less than $100,000, and yet here was my son, who had learned his trade in my office, a young man of good character, and yet unable to find work at his trade because of his color and race. Walking among my fellow-citizens in the street, I have never failed to receive due courtesy and kindness. Some men have even shown an interest in saving my soul; but of what avail are such manifestations where one sees himself ostracized, degraded and denied the means of obtaining his daily bread?

From *The New York Times,* August 8, 1869.

REPRESENTATIVE JEFFERSON LONG

*G*eorgia's whites did not let up *in their war upon the defenseless black man. In the year that led up to the congressional elections of 1869, at least two hundred sixty outrages against the Negro were reported in the state. On election day, the terror climaxed in mob action against Negro voters. Seven were killed and Jefferson Long, the colored candidate for Congress, escaped the lynchers only by hiding in a sewer. The self-educated Long, born a slave, and a tailor by trade, carried his district. No wonder, then, that his first speech in Congress, on February 2, 1871, was a plea for keeping the test-oath requiring voters to uphold the Constitution. His warning went unheeded, and a little later, Congress dropped the test-oath.*

I prophesy trouble . . .
1871

THE OBJECT OF THE BILL before the House is to modify the test-oath. As a citizen of the South, living in Georgia, born and raised in that State, having been there during the war and up to the present time, I know the condition of affairs in that State. Now, sir, we propose here today to modify the test-oath, and to give to those men in the rebel States who are disloyal today to the government this favor. We propose, sir, to remove political disabilities from the very men who were the leaders of the Ku Klux and who have committed midnight outrages in that State.

What do those men say? Before their disabilities are removed they say, "We will remain quiet until all of our disabilities are removed, and then we shall again take the lead." Why, Mr. Speaker, in my State since emancipation there have been over five hundred loyal men shot down by the disloyal men there, and not one of those who took part in committing those outrages has ever been brought to justice. Do we, then, really propose here today, when the country is not ready for it, when those disloyal people still hate this Government, when loyal men dare not carry the "stars and stripes" through our streets, for if they do they will be turned out of employment, to relieve from political disability the very men who have committed these Ku Klux outrages? I think that I am doing my duty to my constituents and my duty to my country when I vote against any such proposition.

Yes, sir; I do mean that murders and outrages are being committed there. I received no longer ago than this morning a letter from a man in my State, a loyal man who was appointed postmaster by the President, stating that he was beaten in the streets a few days ago. I have also received information from the lower part of Georgia that disloyal men went in the midnight disguised and took a loyal man out and shot him; and not one of them has been brought to justice. Loyal men are constantly being cruelly beaten. When we take the men who commit these outrages before judges and juries we find that they are in the hands of the very Ku Klux themselves who protect them.

Mr. Speaker, I propose, as a man raised as a slave, my mother a slave before me, and my ancestry slaves as far back as I can trace them, yet holding no animosity to the law-abiding people of my State, and those who are willing to stand by the Government, while I am willing to remove the disabilities of all such who will support the Government, still I propose for one, knowing the condition of things there in Georgia, not to vote for any modification of the test-oath in favor of disloyal men.

From *Congressional Globe*, 1871.

[From the Independent Monitor, Tuscaloosa, Alabama, September 1, 1868.]

A PROSPECTIVE SCENE IN THE CITY OF OAKS, 4TH OF MARCH, 1869.

" Hang, curs, hang ! * * * * * *Their* complexion is perfect gallows. Stand fast, good
fate, to *their* hanging ! * * * * * If they be not born to be hanged, our case is miserable."

The above cut represents the fate in store for those great pests of Southern society—
the carpet-bagger and scalawag—if found in Dixie's land after the break of day on the
4th of March next.

T*he legal power to punish had
been the slaveholder's primary method of control. The flog-
ging, branding, mutilation, and mob violence commonly reported in slavery days did not end with Emancipation. Violence had been deeply embedded in Southern life and now it
was used to put down all those whom the former Confederates
saw as enemies. Anyone who tried to educate the Negroes on
their political rights and to help them vote, or who preached
Negro-white equality, was a fit target. By 1867 the Ku Klux
Klan and several other secret organizations had combined
their terror in an attempt to destroy Radical Reconstruction
throughout the South. They rode under the banner of white
supremacy. Business pressure, vote-buying, the lash, the torch,*

32

and the gun were their weapons. They meant to crush the Negro and his white allies.

The first selection to follow comes from a transcription, taken many years later, of an ex-slave's reminiscences of the Klan in North Carolina.

If the struggling new governments were to make any headway, they had to fight back. They passed laws against the night riders and with their state militia tried to stop the outrages. But the violence did not let up and their very survival as governments was threatened. Appeals to President Grant for federal intervention brought little relief. When cases were pressed, witnesses were usually too scared to testify, and even if they did, juries refused to convict.

Finally, in April, 1871, Congress passed a law known as the Ku Klux Act which empowered the President to declare martial law where the secret organizations were deemed "in rebellion against the government of the United States." A joint committee of Congress went South to hold hearings on the counter-reconstruction. Negro witnesses by the score told what was happening to their people.

The second selection is part of the testimony on South Carolina which Willis Johnson gave the committee on July 3, 1871.

KKK...

NORTH CAROLINA

AFTER US COLORED FOLKS was 'sidered free and turned loose, the Ku Klux broke out. Some colored people started to farming, like I told you, and gathered the old stock. If they got so they made good money and had a good farm, the Ku Klux would come and murder 'em. The government builded schoolhouses, and the Ku Klux went to work and burned 'em down. They'd go to the jails and take the colored men out and knock their brains out and break their necks and throw 'em in the river.

There was a colored man they taken, his name was Jim Freeman. They taken him and destroyed his stuff and him 'cause he was making some money. Hung him on a tree in his front yard, right in front of his cabin.

There was some colored young men went to the schools they'd opened by the government. Some white woman said someone had stole something of hers, so they put them young men in jail. The Ku Klux went to the jail and took 'em out and killed 'em. That happened the second year after the war.

34

KKK

After the Ku Kluxes got so strong, the colored men got together and made the complaint before the law. The governor told the law to give 'em the old guns in the commissary, what the Southern soldiers had used, so they issued the colored men old muskets and said protect themselves. They got together and organized the militia and had leaders like regular soldiers. They didn't meet 'cept when they heared the Ku Kluxes were coming to get some colored folks. Then they was ready for 'em. They'd hide in the cabins, and then's when they found out who a lot of them Ku Kluxes was, 'cause a lot of 'em was kilt. They wore long sheets and covered the hosses with sheets so you couldn't recognize 'em. Men you thought was your friend was Ku Kluxes, and you'd deal with 'em in stores in the daytime, and at night they'd come out to your house and kill you. I never took part in none of the fights, but I heared the others talk 'bout them, but not where them Ku Kluxes could hear 'em.

From *Lay My Burden Down,* edited by B. A. Botkin,
University of Chicago Press, 1945.

SOUTH CAROLINA

When I awoke, as near as I can tell, it was between 12 and 1 o'clock. I heard some one call "Sims." I held still and listened, and heard them walk from his door to my door. I was upstairs, and I got up and came downstairs. They walked back to his house again and asked him to put his head out. He did not answer, but his wife asked them who they were. They said they were friends. They walked back to my door again, and just as they got to the door they blew a whistle. Another whistle off a piece answered, and then men seemed to surround the house and all parts of the yard. Then they hallooed, "Open the door."

I said nothing. I went to the head of the bed and got my pistol, and leaned forward on the table with the pistol just at the door. They tried with several surges to get the door open, but it did not come open. They went to the wood-pile and got the axe, and struck the front-door some licks, bursted it open, and then went to the back door and burst it open. Nobody had yet come into the house. They said, "Strike a light." Then I dropped down on my knees back of the table, and they struck some matches and threw them in the house, and two of them stepped in the front door, and that brought them within arm's length of me as they stood there. As soon as they did that, I raised my pistol quickly, right up one's back, and shot, and he fell and hallooed, and the other tried to pull him out. As he pulled him I shot again. As they were pulling, others ran up and pulled him out in the yard, and when the whole party was out in the yard I stepped to the door and shot again, and then jumped to the back door and ran.

I got off. I stayed away until the next morning; then I came back and tracked them half a mile where they had toted this man and laid him down. I was afraid to go further. Mr. Sims and I were together, and I would not go any further, and he told me to go away, that I ought not to stay there, that he saw the men and saw the wounded man, and was satisfied that he was dead or mortally wounded, and I must leave.

Mr. John Calmes, the candidate of the Democrats for the legislature, advised me to take a paper and go around the settlement to the white people, stating that I would never vote the radical ticket, and he said he did not think they would interfere with me then. He said that all they had against me was

KKK

that on election day I took the tickets around among the black people; and he said: "You knocked me out of a good many votes, but you are a good fellow and a good laborer, and we want labor in this country." I told him I would not do that. . . .

From Testimony Taken by the Joint Select Committee to Inquire Into the Condition of Affairs in the Late Insurrectionary States.

PROCEEDINGS

OF THE

STATE CONVENTION

OF

The Colored Citizens

OF

TENNESSEE,

HELD IN NASHVILLE,

Feb. 22d, 23d, 24th & 25th 1871.

C. LeRoi, Printer, 14 N. College St.

1871

Reconstruction has often been called the era of "Negro rule." How mistaken this is can be seen from a quick look at a few facts. Most Negro officeholders of the Reconstruction served in local and state governments. Only twenty-two sat in Congress between 1869 and 1901. Two of these represented Mississippi in the Senate; the rest were in the lower house. Most served only one or two terms. Only two, Joseph Rainey and Robert Smalls, served five. All had not only the powerful opposition of the white Democrats to contend with, but found many whites in their own Republican Party just as determined to keep political power for themselves. With important committee posts closed to them, the twenty-two Negro members of Congress could have little influence on lawmaking.

In the state governments, too, Negroes never held control. They won high office and made large contributions to public life, but they never dominated or ruled any state in the South. Their greatest numerical strength was in South Carolina. In the first Reconstruction legislature the Negroes held eighty-seven seats and the whites forty. But whites always controlled the state senate and the governorship.

Among these whites were two groups, called "carpetbaggers" and "scalawags." The first term was used against the Northerners who were in the South during Reconstruction. It was a label that implied empty-handed, greedy men had come down to grab the belongings of Southerners and stuff them into their carpetbags. Certainly there were such dishonest Northerners bent on exploiting the South. But thousands of others settled in the South after the war to help the freedmen and to build democracy. Often theirs was a strong influence on politics because they had both the education and experience that the freedmen and the loyal Southern whites lacked, and they had, too, the support of the party in power in Washington.

Alongside these "carpetbaggers" stood the "scalawags"— Southern whites who had opposed secession and hated the rich planters who had led the Confederate cause. Because they took part in the new Reconstruction program they were reviled by the former Confederates. It was these three groups— the Negro, the Northern white and the loyal Southern white —who figured in the Reconstruction governments. The Negro was never dominant.

The largest number of Negroes to be sent to Congress from any one state came from South Carolina. One of them, Joseph Rainey, was the first Negro to be elected to Congress. Born in slavery, his freedom—and his whole family's—had been purchased by the earnings of his father, a barber. Joseph too became a barber in Charleston and had his private schooling there. Forced to work on Confederate fortifications when the war began, he fled to the West Indies. He returned when the war was over and was elected to the state constitutional convention and then the state senate before going to Congress. On March 5, 1872, he rose in Congress to make this answer to attacks on "Negro rule" in his state.

We did not discriminate . . .

1872

Now, SIR, I have not time to vindicate fully the course of action of the colored people of South Carolina. We are certainly in the majority there; I admit that we are as two to one. Sir, I ask this House, I ask the country, I ask white men, I ask Democrats, I ask Republicans whether the Negroes have presumed to take improper advantage of the majority they hold in that State by disregarding the interest of the minority? They have not. Our convention which met in 1868, and in which the Negroes were in a large majority, did not pass any proscriptive or disfranchising acts, but adopted a liberal constitution, securing alike equal rights to all citizens, white and black, male and female, as far as possible. Mark you, we did not discriminate, although we had a majority.

Our constitution towers up in its majesty with provisions for the equal protection of all classes of citizens. Notwithstanding our majority there, we have never attempted to deprive any man in that State of the rights and immunities to which he is entitled under the Constitution of this Government. You cannot point to me a single act passed by our Legislature, at any time, which had a tendency to reflect upon or oppress any white citizen of South Carolina. You cannot show me one enactment by which the majority in our State have undertaken to crush the white men because the latter are in a minority.

From *Congressional Globe,* 1872.

FREEDMEN'S SCHOOL AT ATLANTA, GEORGIA

One goal of the Freedmen's Bureau was to establish schools in the South. In its five short years of life, with the help of religious and philanthropic groups, it founded 4,300 schools, from the elementary grades through college. With tuition free, and often schoolbooks too, over a quarter of a million Negroes were able to start their education. Early in the Civil War, when the Sea Islands off South Carolina had been captured by the Union forces, Yankee schoolmarms had headed South to teach Negro children and adults to read and write. The institution of slavery had kept back the development of the Negro people, and the abolitionist and missionary teachers hoped to demonstrate that the widely held notions—in the North as well as in the South —of the inherent superiority and inferiority of races, were wrong. Slave codes had forbidden the Negroes education, and the vast majority were therefore illiterate. The teachers were joyously welcomed by them everywhere. Within a few years some schools had progressed so rapidly that they were training Negroes to go out and teach.

Probably a majority of the teachers who came South were abolitionists. These veterans of the antislavery crusade were also the backbone of the freedmen's aid societies that helped raise funds, recruit teachers, write textbooks, and open the schools in the South. Their zeal was notable, and necessary, for they had to overcome many obstacles in the first years of freedom. One was the fact that the children were raised in homes almost completely without cultural stimulus. They knew little or nothing of the world beyond the plantation or the village boundaries. Many had never seen a book or newspaper; some did not know right from left, or had no concept of time. Yet they learned to read, well and swiftly, under the guidance of teachers who cared.

But it was outside the school walls that the greatest barrier to education stood. It was the grim resolve of many Southern whites that these "aliens," these Yankee schoolteachers, should not meddle with "their" Negroes. The "nigger teachers," as they were called, were suspected of spreading notions of political and social equality. They were often ostracized, insulted, whipped, and their schoolhouses burned.

Perhaps one of the best-known instances of the Negro's powerful desire for education is the story of Booker T. Washington. Born a slave in Virginia, he never slept in a bed or ate at a table until after Emancipation. In his autobiography, Up From Slavery, *he tells how he used* Webster's Speller *to teach himself to read, and attended the first colored school opened in the neighborhood by a Northern Negro. For five years, from the age of nine, he worked from 4:00 A.M. to 9:00 A.M. in a coal mine, went to school, and returned to the mine for another two hours. In the passage that follows, he describes how he got to Hampton Institute.*

I had reached the promised land . . .
1872

ONE DAY, while at work in the coal-mine, I happened to overhear two miners talking about a great school for coloured people somewhere in Virginia. This was the first time that I had ever heard anything about any kind of school or college that was more pretentious than the little coloured school in our town.

In the darkness of the mine I noiselessly crept as close as I could to the two men who were talking. I heard one tell the other that not only was the school established for the members of my race, but that opportunities were provided by which poor but worthy students could work out all or a part of the cost of board, and at the same time be taught some trade or industry.

As they went on describing the school, it seemed to me that it must be the greatest place on earth, and not even Heaven presented more attractions for me at that time than did the Hampton Normal and Agricultural Institute in Virginia about which these men were talking. I resolved at once to go to that school, although I had no idea where it was, or how many miles away, or how I was going to reach it; I remembered only that I was on fire constantly with one ambition, and that was to go to Hampton. This thought was with me day and night. . . .

In the fall of 1872 I determined to make an effort to get there, although, as I have stated, I had no definite idea of the direction in which Hampton was, or of what it would cost to go there. I do not think that any one thoroughly sympathized with me in my ambition to go to Hampton unless it was my mother, and she was troubled with a grave fear that I was starting out on a "wild-goose chase." At any rate, I got only a half-hearted consent from her that I might start. The small amount of money that I had earned had been consumed by my stepfather and the remainder of the family, with the exception of a very few dollars, and so I had very little with which to buy clothes and pay my travelling expenses. My brother John helped me all that he could, but of course that was not a great deal, for his work was in the coal-mine, where he did not earn much, and most of what he did earn went in the direction of paying the household expenses.

Perhaps the thing that touched and pleased me most in connection with my starting for Hampton was the interest that many of the older coloured people took in the matter. They had spent the best days of their lives in slavery, and hardly expected to live to see the time when they would see a member of their race leave home to attend a boarding-school. Some of these older people would give me a nickel, others a quarter, or a handkerchief.

Finally the great day came, and I started for Hampton. I had only a small, cheap satchel that contained what few articles of clothing I could get. My mother at the time was rather weak and broken in health. I hardly expected to see her again, and thus our parting was all the more sad. She, however, was very brave through it all. At that time there were no through trains connecting that part of West Virginia with eastern Virginia. Trains ran only a portion of the way, and the remainder of the distance was travelled by stage-coaches.

The distance from Malden to Hampton is about five hundred miles. I had not been away from home many hours before it began to grow painfully evident that I did not have enough money to pay my fare to Hampton. . . .

By walking, begging rides both in wagons and in the cars, in some way, after a number of days, I reached the city of Richmond, Virginia, about eighty-two miles from Hampton. When I reached there, tired, hungry, and dirty, it was late in the night. I had never been in a large city, and this rather added to my misery . . . I was completely out of money. . . .

I must have walked the streets till after midnight. At last I became so exhausted that I could walk no longer. I was tired, I was hungry, I was everything but discouraged. Just about the time when I reached extreme physical exhaustion, I came upon a portion of a street where the board sidewalk was considerably elevated. I waited for a few minutes, till I was sure that no passers-by could see me, and then crept under the sidewalk and lay for the night upon the ground, with my satchel of clothing for a pillow. Nearly all night I could hear the tramp of feet over my head. The next morning I found myself somewhat refreshed, but I was extremely hungry, because it had been a long time since I had had sufficient food. As soon as it became light enough for me to see my surroundings I noticed that I was near a large ship, and that this ship seemed to be unloading a cargo of pig iron. I went at once to the vessel and asked the captain to permit me to help unload the vessel in order to get money for food. The captain, a white man, who seemed to be kind-hearted, consented. I worked long enough to earn money for my breakfast, and it seems to me, as I remember it now, to have been about the best breakfast that I have ever eaten.

My work pleased the captain so well that he told me if I desired I could continue working for a small amount per day. This I was very glad to do. I continued working on this vessel for a number of days. After buying food with the small wages I received there was not much left to add to the amount I must get to pay my way to Hampton. In order to economize in every way possible, so as to be sure to reach Hampton in a reasonable time, I continued to sleep under the same sidewalk that gave me shelter the first night I was in Richmond. . . .

When I had saved what I considered enough money with which to reach Hampton, I thanked the captain of the vessel for his kindness, and started again. Without any unusual occurrence I reached Hampton, with a surplus of exactly fifty cents with which to begin my education. To me it had been a long, eventful journey; but the first sight of the large, three-story, brick school building seemed to have rewarded me for all that I had undergone in order to reach the place. . . . It seemed to me to be the largest and most beautiful building I had ever seen. The sight of it seemed to give me new life. I felt that a new kind of existence had now begun—that life would now have a new meaning. I felt that I had reached the promised land, and I resolved to let no obstacle prevent me from putting forth the highest effort to fit myself to accomplish the most good in the world. . . .

Life at Hampton was a constant revelation to me; was constantly taking me into a new world. The matter of having meals at regular hours, of eating on a tablecloth, using a napkin, the use of the bath-tub and of the tooth-brush, as well as the use of sheets upon the bed, were all new to me. . . .

The charge for my board at Hampton was ten dollars per month. I was expected to pay a part of this in cash and to work out the remainder. To meet this cash payment, as I have stated, I had just fifty cents when I reached the institution. Aside from a very few dollars that my brother John was able to send me once in a while, I had no money with which to pay my board. I was determined from the first to make my work as janitor so valuable that my services would be indispensable. This I succeeded in doing to such an extent that I was soon informed that I would be allowed the full cost of my board in return for my work. The cost of tuition was seventy dollars a year. This, of course, was wholly beyond my ability to provide. If I had been compelled to pay the seventy dollars for tuition, in addition to providing for my board, I would have been compelled to leave the Hampton school. General Armstrong, however, very kindly got Mr. S. Griffitts Morgan, of New Bedford, Mass., to defray the cost of my tuition during the whole time that I was at Hampton. . . .

After having been for a while at Hampton, I found myself in difficulty because I did not have books and clothing. Usually, however, I got around the trouble about books by borrowing from those who were more fortunate than myself. As to clothes, when I reached Hampton I had practically nothing.

Everything that I possessed was in a small hand satchel. . . .

In some way I managed to get on till the teachers learned that I was in earnest and meant to succeed, and then some of them were kind enough to see that I was partly supplied with second-hand clothing that had been sent in barrels from the North. These barrels proved a blessing to hundreds of poor but deserving students. Without them I question whether I should ever have gotten through Hampton. . . .

I was among the youngest of the students who were in Hampton at that time. Most of the students were men and women—some as old as forty years of age. As I now recall the scene of my first year, I do not believe that one often has the opportunity of coming into contact with three or four hundred men and women who were so tremendously in earnest as these men and women were. Every hour was occupied in study or work. Nearly all had had enough actual contact with the world to teach them the need of education. Many of the older ones were, of course, too old to master the text-books very thoroughly, and it was often sad to watch their struggles; but they made up in earnestness much of what they lacked in books. Many of them were as poor as I was, and, besides having to wrestle with their books, they had to struggle with a poverty which prevented their having the necessities of life. Many of them had aged parents who were dependent upon them, and some of them were men who had wives whose support in some way they had to provide for.

The great and prevailing idea that seemed to take possession of every one was to prepare himself to lift up the people at his home. No one seemed to think of himself. And the officers and teachers, what a rare set of human beings they were! They worked for the students night and day, in season and out of season. They seemed happy only when they were helping students in some manner. Whenever it is written—and I hope it will be—the part that the Yankee teachers played in the education of the Negroes immediately after the war will make one of the most thrilling parts of the history of this country.

From *Up From Slavery,* by Booker T. Washington, 1900.

A POPULAR LITHOGRAPH OF THE 1880's, PAYING
SPECIAL TRIBUTE TO THE VALUE OF EDUCATION

N*egroes in the South had been
denied education before the Civil War, whether they could
pay for it or not. As for the whites, usually only those who
could afford private schools or tutoring were educated. There
were almost no public schools. In the first postwar years, the
former Confederate states adopted education laws, but, as a
Louisiana legislator said, only for "the superior race of men—
the White race." Just as they limited the vote to whites, so they
limited schooling to whites. The Negro kept illiterate in slavery
was to stay illiterate in freedom if the Old South was to have
its way.*

But when the Stevens-Sumner Republicans in Congress put through Radical Reconstruction, new and progressive constitutions were written in each state by the black and white delegates. The poor whites joined with the Negroes to establish a system of universal public education. They knew all must be educated to meet the responsibilities of citizenship intelligently. And so, against the opposition of upper-class whites who feared the tax burden, they provided for free education.

Would Negroes and whites be educated together? The question of mixed schools was hotly debated. The Southern whites usually opposed it. Northern whites now sitting in Southern assemblies had come from states where very few schools were integrated. They did not press the issue. But the Negroes spoke up for integration because they believed segregated schools were constitutionally undemocratic and would inevitably lead to inferior education for Negroes.

Most of the states avoided the issue by saying nothing about it in the clauses on education. Only two, South Carolina and Louisiana, wrote integrated schooling into their constitutions and in both, separate schools returned in practice by the 1870's.

The case for integrated schooling was put with his usual power and clarity in an article Frederick Douglass published on May 2, 1872, in his newspaper, The New National Era.

We want mixed schools . . .

1872

THE QUESTION of the establishment of common schools in the District of Columbia in which caste prejudices will not be nurtured, is now agitating the people of this community. A large and enthusiastic meeting of those friendly to the mixed school measure presented in the Senate by the Hon. Chas. Sumner, was held in Union League Hall last week. We hope for the speedy passage of the bill of Mr. Sumner's, in order that the mad current of prejudice against the Negro may be checked; and also that the baleful influence upon the children of the colored race of being taught by separation from the whites that the whites are superior to them may be destroyed.

Throughout the South all the schools should be mixed. From our observations during a trip to the South we are convinced that the interests of the poor whites and the colored people are identical. Both are ignorant, and both are the tools of designing educated white men; and the poor whites are more particularly used to further schemes opposed to their own best interests. In that section everything that will bring the poor white man and the colored man closer together should be done; they should be taught to make common cause against the rich land-holders of the South who never regarded a poor white man of as much importance as they did slaves. Educate the poor white children and the colored children together; let them grow up to know that color makes no difference as to the rights of a man; that both the black man and the white man are at home; that the country is as much the country of one as of the other, and that both together must make it a valuable country.

Now in the South the poor white man is taught that he is better than the black man, and not as good as the 250,000 slaveholders of former days; the result is that the slaveholders command the poor white man to murder the black man, to burn down his school-houses, and to in every conceivable manner maltreat him, and the command is obeyed. This tends to make the ex-slaveholder more powerful, and is of no good to the poor white who is really as much despised as the Negro. The cunning ex-slaveholder sets those who should be his enemies to fighting each other and thus diverts attention from himself. Educate the colored children and white children together in your day and night schools throughout the South, and they will learn to know each other better, and be better able to co-operate for mutual benefit.

We want mixed schools not because our colored schools are inferior to white schools—not because colored instructors are inferior to white instructors, but because we want to do away with a system that exalts one class and debases another. . . .

Our idea of mixed schools comprehends the employment of

colored as well as white teachers, and of neither unless they are competent. Anything less than this would be fostering the very caste distinctions of which we all complain. It is saying to the colored child you may learn and acquire an abundance of intelligence but you must never hope to know enough to be able to teach a primary school composed of white children and colored children. . . . We look to mixed schools to teach that worth and ability are to be the criterion of manhood and not race and color.

From *The New National Era,* May 2, 1872.

Negroes were citizens entitled to equal treatment before the law. So the new Fourteenth Amendment to the Constitution said. But it was all too plain that few people were paying any attention to it. In 1872-1873 Congress tried again, this time spelling it out and confining the application to the District of Columbia. It passed laws providing that a "respectable well-behaved" person had to be served without regard to race, color, or previous condition of servitude by proprietors of hotels and other public places in the nation's capital.

Still, racial segregation persisted. Whites were resolved to keep the Negro in an inferior position. Racial separation was a means to that end. Senator Charles Sumner of Massachusetts, one of the few Radical Republicans remaining in Congress who were still militantly outspoken, worked hard for adoption of a federal civil rights law, but met defeat again and again. In

March of 1875 enough strength was finally mustered to pass the bill.

The new Civil Rights Act gave citizens of every race and color the right to equal treatment in inns, public conveyances, theaters, and other places of public amusement. But in the trading that took place to get the needed votes, some of the bill's key provisions, including desegregation of the schools, were knocked out.

Several Negro congressmen took part in the debate on the measure. One was James T. Rapier of Alabama, a freeborn Negro who had studied law in Canada for eight years. He was admitted to the bar, taught school, and travelled as a correspondent for a Northern newspaper. He was prominent in Alabama's constitutional convention. By the time he was elected to the 43rd Congress (1873-1875), the Democrats were taking back political control of his state. Reconstruction in Alabama was to last less than seven years.

In his speech, Rapier describes segregation on railroads and in hotels and restaurants, and answers arguments against the Civil Rights Bill.

Is the Negro a man? . . .

1873

THERE IS NOT AN INN between Washington and Montgomery, a distance of more than a thousand miles, that will accommodate me to a bed or meal. Now, then, is there a man upon this floor who is so heartless, whose breast is so void of the better feelings, as to say that this brutal custom needs no regulation? I hold that it does and that Congress is the body to regulate it. Authority for its action is found not only in the fourteenth amendment to the Constitution, but by virtue of that amendment (which makes all persons born here citizens) authority is found in article 4, section 2, of the Federal Constitution, which declares in positive language "that the citizens of each State shall have the same rights as the citizens of the several States." . . .

Sir, I submit that I am degraded as long as I am denied the public privileges common to other men, and that the members of this House are correspondingly degraded by recognizing my political equality while I occupy such a humiliating position. What a singular attitude for lawmakers of this great nation to assume, rather come down to me than allow me to go up to them. . . .

Sir, there is a cowardly propensity in the human heart that delights in oppressing somebody else, and in the gratification of this base desire we always select a victim that can be outraged with safety. As a general thing, the Jew has been the subject in most parts of the world; but here the Negro is the most available for this purpose; for this reason in part he was seized upon, and not because he is naturally inferior to any one else. Instead of his enemies believing him to be incapable of a high order of mental culture, they have shown that they believe the reverse to be true, by taking the most elaborate pains to prevent his development. And the smaller the caliber of the white man the more frantically has he fought to prevent the intellectual and moral progress of the Negro, for the simple but good reason that he has most to fear from such a result. He does not wish to see the Negro approach the high moral standard of a man and gentleman. . . .

Sir, in order that I might know something of the feelings of a freeman, a privilege denied me in the land of my birth, I left home last year and traveled six months in foreign lands, and the moment I put my foot upon the deck of a ship that unfurled a foreign flag from its mast-head, distinctions on account of my color ceased. I am not aware that my presence on board the steamer put her off her course. I believe we made the trip in the usual time. It was in other countries than my own that I was not a stranger, that I could approach a hotel without the fear that the door would be slammed in my face. Sir, I feel this humiliation very keenly; it dwarfs my manhood, and certainly it impairs my usefulness as a citizen. . . .

After all, this question resolves itself to this: either I am a man or I am not a man. If one, I am entitled to all the rights, privileges, and immunities common to any other class in this country; if not a man, I have no right to vote, no right to a seat here; if no right to vote, then 20 per cent of the members on this floor have no right here, but, on the contrary, hold their seats in violation of law. If the Negro has no right to vote, then one-eighth of your Senate consists of members who have no shadow of a claim to the places they occupy; and . . . a half-dozen governors in the South figure as usurpers.

This is the legitimate conclusion of the argument that the Negro is not a man and is not entitled to all the public rights common to other men, and you cannot escape it. But when I press my claims I am asked, "Is it good policy?" My answer is, "Policy is out of the question; it has nothing to do with it; that you can have no policy in dealing with your citizens; that there must be one law for all; that in this case justice is the only standard to be used, and you can no more divide justice than you can divide Deity." On the other hand, I am told that I must respect the prejudices of others. Now, sir, no one respects reasonable and intelligent prejudice more than I. I respect religious prejudices, for example; these I can comprehend. But how can I have respect for the prejudices that prompt a man to turn up his nose at the males of a certain race, while at the same time he has a fondness for the females of the same race to the extent of cohabitation? Out of four poor unfortunate colored women, who from poverty were forced to go to the lying-in branch of the Freedman's Hospital here in the District last year, three gave birth to children whose fathers were white men, and I venture to say that if they were members of this body, would vote against the civil rights bill. Do you, can you wonder at my want of respect for this kind of prejudice? To make me feel uncomfortable appears to be the highest ambition of many white men. It is to them a positive luxury, which they seek to indulge at every opportunity. . . .

Sir, this whole thing grows out of a desire to establish a system of "caste," an anti-republican principle, in our free country. In Europe they have princes, dukes, lords, etc., in contradistinction to the middle classes and peasants. Further East they have the brahmans or priests, who rank above the sudras or laborers. In those countries distinctions are based upon blood and position. . . .

Our distinction is color . . . and our lines are much broader than anything they know of. Here a drunken white man is not only equal to a drunken Negro (as would be the case anywhere else), but superior to the most sober and orderly one; here an ignorant white man is not only the equal of an unlettered Negro, but is superior to the most cultivated. . . .

Mr. Speaker, to call this land the asylum of the oppressed is a misnomer, for upon all sides I am treated as a pariah. I hold that the solution of this whole matter is to enact such laws and prescribe such penalties for their violation as will prevent any person from discriminating against another in public places on account of color. No one asks, no one seeks the passage of a law that will interfere with any one's private affairs. But I do ask the enactment of a law to secure me in the enjoyment of public privileges. But when I ask this I am told that I must wait for public opinion; that it is a matter that cannot be forced by law. While I admit that public opinion is a power, and in many cases is a law of itself, yet I cannot lose sight of the fact that both statute law and the law of necessity manufacture public opinion.

I remember, it was unpopular to enlist Negro soldiers in our late war, and after they enlisted it was equally unpopular to have them fight in the same battles; but when it became a necessity in both cases, public opinion soon came around to that point. No white father objected to the Negro's becoming food for powder if thereby his son could be saved. No white woman objected to the Negro marching in the same ranks and fighting in the same battles if by that her husband could escape burial in our savannas and return to her and her little ones.

Suppose there had been no reconstruction acts nor amendments to the Constitution, when would public opinion in the South have suggested the propriety of giving me the ballot? Unaided by law when would public opinion have prompted the Administration to appoint members of my race to represent this Government at foreign courts? It is said by some well-meaning men that the colored man has now every right under the common law; in reply I wish to say that that kind of law commands very little respect when applied to the rights of colored men in my portion of the country; the only law that we have any regard for is uncommon law of the most positive character. And I repeat, if you will place upon your statute-books laws that will protect me in my rights, that public opinion will speedily follow.

From *Congressional Globe*, 1873.

ROBERT B. ELLIOTT DELIVERING HIS GREAT SPEECH ON CIVIL RIGHTS

T*he little old man with the long · white hair and the dead-white skin speaking to the Congress was Mr. Alexander Stephens of Georgia, the former vice president of the Confederacy. Now, his leadership in the slaveholders' rebellion forgiven, he was back in the seat he had held for many terms before the war. When he finished his attack on the Civil Rights Bill, the word spread rapidly through Washington that on the next day he would be answered by a Negro, the brilliant Robert Brown Elliott.*

Born in Boston and educated in England at Eton, Elliott had studied law in London and come to South Carolina to practice. He had mastered several languages and collected one of the finest private libraries in the state. He helped write the state constitution and was elected to the legislative assembly at twenty-six. By twenty-eight, he was serving in the United States House of Representatives.

When the handsome, dark-skinned congressman rose to speak on January, 6, 1874, the floor of the House and the galleries were packed. Senators too were there to watch the dramatic confrontation between "Anglo-Saxon and the undoubted African," as one observer put it. When the eloquent speech was ended, great applause rolled over the chamber. Even his political enemies were impressed.

Before his term was up, Elliott resigned and returned home, believing state politics were a better arena. He became speaker of South Carolina's assembly. Two Negroes had risen to the lieutenant-governorship of the state, and it was said Elliott meant to become the country's first Negro governor. But his hopes ended when Reconstruction was overthrown in South Carolina, too, by 1876.

Justice demands it . . .

1874

IT IS A MATTER of regret to me
that it is necessary at this day that I should rise in the presence
of an American Congress to advocate a bill which simply as-
serts equal rights and equal public privileges for all classes of
American citizens. I regret, sir, that the dark hue of my skin
may lend a color to the imputation that I am controlled by
motives personal to myself in my advocacy of this great measure of a national justice. Sir, the motive that impels me is re-
stricted by no such narrow boundary, but is as broad as your
Constitution. I advocate it, sir, because it is right. . . .

In the events that led to the achievement of American independence the Negro was not an inactive or unconcerned spec-
tator. He bore his part bravely upon many battle-fields, although uncheered by that certain hope of political elevation
which victory would secure to the white man. The tall granite
shaft, which a grateful State has reared above its sons who
fell in defending Fort Griswold against the attack of Benedict

Arnold, bears the name of Jordan, Freeman, and other brave men of the African race who there cemented with their blood the corner-stone of the Republic. In the State which I have the honor in part to represent the rifle of the black man rang out against the troops of the British crown in the darkest days of the American Revolution. . . .

At the battle of New Orleans, under the immortal Jackson, a colored regiment held the extreme right of the American line unflinchingly, and drove back the British column that pressed upon them, at the point of the bayonet. So marked was their valor on that occasion that it evoked from their great commander the warmest encomiums, as will be seen from his dispatch announcing the brilliant victory. . . .

But, sir, we are told by the distinguished gentleman from Georgia [Mr. Alexander Stephens] that Congress has no power under the Constitution to pass such a law, and that the passage of such an act is in direct contravention of the rights of the States. I cannot assent to any such proposition. The constitution of a free government ought always to be construed in favor of human rights. Indeed, the thirteenth, fourteenth, and fifteenth amendments, in positive words, invest Congress with the power to protect the citizen in his civil and political rights. . . .

Are we then, sir, with the amendments to our Constitution staring us in the face, with these grand truths of history before our eyes, with innumerable wrongs daily inflicted upon five million citizens demanding redress, to commit this question to the diversity of State legislation? . . .

These amendments, one and all . . . have as their all-pervading design and end the security to the recently enslaved race, not only their nominal freedom, but their complete pro-

tection from those who had formerly exercised unlimited do-
minion over them. It is in this broad light that all these amendments must be read, the purpose to secure the perfect equality
before the law of all citizens of the United States. What you
give to one class you must give to all; what you deny to one
class you shall deny to all, unless in the exercise of the common
and universal police power of the State you find it needful to
confer exclusive privileges on certain citizens, to be held and
exercised still for the common good of all. . . .

There are privileges and immunities which belong to me as
a citizen of the United States, and there are other privileges
and immunities which belong to me as a citizen of my State.
The former are under the protection of the Constitution and
laws of the United States, and the latter are under the protection of the constitution and laws of my State. But what of that?
Are the rights which I now claim—the right to enjoy the common public conveniences of travel on public highways, of rest
and refreshment at public inns, of education in public schools,
of burial in public cemeteries—rights which I hold as a citizen
of the United States or of my State? Or, to state the question
more exactly, is not the denial of such privileges to me a denial
to me of the equal protection of the laws? For it is under this
clause of the fourteenth amendment that we place the present
bill, no State shall "deny to any person within its jurisdiction
the equal protection of the laws." No matter, therefore,
whether his rights are held under the United States or under his
particular State, he is equally protected by this amendment. He
is always and everywhere entitled to the equal protection of the
laws. All discrimination is forbidden; and while the rights of
citizens of a State as such are not defined or conferred by the

Constitution of the United States, yet all discrimination, all denials of equality before the law, all denial of the equal protection of the laws, whether State or national laws, is forbidden.

The distinction between the two kinds of citizenship is clear, and the Supreme Court have clearly pointed out this distinction, but they have nowhere written a word or line which denies to Congress the power to prevent a denial of equality of rights, whether those rights exist by virtue of citizenship of the United States or of a State. Let honorable members mark well this distinction. There are rights which are conferred on us by the United States. There are other rights conferred on us by the States of which we are individually the citizens. The fourteenth amendment does not forbid a State to deny to all its citizens any of those rights which the State itself has conferred, with certain exceptions, which are pointed out in the decision which we are examining. What it does forbid is inequality, is discrimination, or, to use the words of the amendment itself, is the denial "to any person within its jurisdiction the equal protection of the laws."

If a State denies to me rights which are common to all her other citizens, she violates this amendment, unless she can show . . . that she does it in the legitimate exercise of her police power. If she abridges the rights of all her citizens equally, unless those rights are specially guarded by the Constitution of the United States, she does not violate this amendment. This is not to put the rights which I hold by virtue of my citizenship of South Carolina under the protection of the national Government; it is not to blot out or overlook in the slightest particular the distinction between rights held under the United States and the rights held under the States; but it seeks to secure equality, to prevent discrimination, to confer as complete and ample protection on the humblest as on the highest. . . .

If the States . . . continue to deny to any person within their jurisdiction the equal protection of the laws, or as the Supreme Court has said, "deny equal justice in its courts," then Congress is here said to have power to enforce the constitutional guarantee by appropriate legislation. That is the power which this bill now seeks to put in exercise. It proposes to enforce the constitutional guarantee against inequality and discrimination by appropriate legislation. It does not seek to confer new rights, nor to place rights conferred by State citizenship under the protection of the United States, but simply to prevent and forbid inequality and discrimination on account of race, color, or previous condition of servitude. Never was there a bill more completely within the constitutional power of Congress. Never was there a bill which appealed for support more strongly to that sense of justice and fairplay which has been said, and in the main with justice, to be a characteristic of the Anglo-Saxon race. The Constitution warrants it; the Supreme Court sanctions it; justice demands it.

From *Congressional Record*, 1874.

The Negroes who came out of slavery knew well that the source of their old masters' power had been their ownership of the land. Very soon after Emancipation, the freedmen voiced the hope that their new liberty would be rooted deep in a plot of ground they could call their own. They had tilled their native soil for generations, putting their sweat and blood into other men's profit and ease. Now that slavery was dead, they believed they had a right to a piece of land on which they could support their families.

During the war, Congress passed confiscation laws providing that property could be seized for treason, but only during the lifetime of the owner. Some of these lands were sold in lots but often open competition put the moneyless freedmen out of the bidding.

The federal government stumbled towards the future with no clear solutions for the enormous problems of the freedmen. It made vague and often contradictory promises and reneged on many of them. In the end, Reconstruction brought no real change in the economic relations of the South. The Congress and the state legislatures did not face up to redistribution of the land. And when Reconstruction faltered to its end, the small class of planters who had owned most of the land before the war still sat atop their rich acres.

If the Negro farmer was to live, he had to work for others. So he went back into cotton and tobacco and rice and sugar, living under the rule of the planter, still lord of the manor. There was no breakup of the plantation system, either during Reconstruction or after. Instead of slave labor, there was now day labor, or tenant farming and sharecropping. These were changes, to be sure, but to the freedmen life did not feel much different from slavery. The law was made by the planter—especially as the Reconstruction governments were forced out—and for the planter, and when the law did not suffice, he used force to gain his ends.

What sharecropping meant to the freedman is told by three Negroes who gave their affidavit on August 3, 1875, to a congressional committee investigating conditions in Caddo Parish, Louisiana.

You all must live agreeable . . .

1875

WE WORKED, or made a contract to work, and make a crop on shares on Mr. McMoring's place, and worked for one-third of the crop, and he was to find us all of our provisions; and in July, 1875, we was working alone in the field, and Mr. McMoring and McBounton came to us and says, "Well, boys, you all got to get away from here; and that they had gone as far as they could go, and you all must live agreeable, or you shall take what follows"; and the two white men went and got sticks and guns, and told us that we must leave the place; and we told them that we would not leave it, because we don't want to give up our crop for nothing; and they told us that we had better leave, or we would not get anything; and we wanted justice, but he would not let us have justice; and we told them that we would get judges to judge the crop, to say what it is worth; and the white men told us that no judge should come on his place; and we did not want to leave the place, but they beat Isaiah Fuller, and whipped him, and then we got afraid, and we left the place; and we got about thirty acres in cotton, and the best cotton crop in that part of the parish; and we have about twenty-nine acres of corn, and about the best corn in the parish, and it is ripe, and the fodder ready to pull, and our cotton laid by; and runned us off from the place, and told us not to come back any more; and we were due McMoring the sum of one hundred and eighty dollars and they told us that if they ever heard of it any more that they would fix us; and all the time that we were living and working on the place they would not half feed us; and we had to pay for all, or half of our rashings, or what we had to eat, and that is all that we due them for; and we worked for them as though we were slaves, and then treated like dogs all the time.

From Executive Document No. 30,
44th Congress, 2nd Session (Serial No. 1755).

A notorious and turbulent Negro."
This is the obituary some white historians of Mississippi's
Reconstruction era wrote for Charles Caldwell, one of the five
Negroes who sat in the state senate.

Caldwell, a blacksmith born a slave, was lured into a cellar,
wounded in the head by a hidden assassin, dragged up into the
street, and shot to death by a gang of whites on Christmas Day,
1875.

It happened in Clinton, a village in Hinds County, twelve miles from Jackson. In a sense it marked the end of Reconstruction in Mississippi. The "legal" finish had taken place the month before at the polls, when the old rulers of Mississippi ousted the Republicans and took control once again of the state government. The campaign that produced that "victory" was characterized by President Grant in these words: "Mississippi is governed today by officials chosen through fraud and violence such as would scarcely be credited to savages, much less to a civilized and Christian people."

Charles Caldwell was one of the many Mississippi Negroes who emerged from slavery to try for the first time to shape their own future. He was one of the sixteen Negro delegates to the state constitutional convention of 1868, and helped erect the foundations of what the freedmen hoped would be a democratic government.

That same year, on the streets of Jackson, the white son of a judge tried to shoot Caldwell down. Caldwell fired back and killed his attacker. Tried by an all-white jury, he was acquitted on the ground of self-defense—the first Negro ever to kill a white in Mississippi and go free.

He became one of the two Negroes on the county board of police, serving until elected to the senate of the first Reconstruction legislature in 1870. Throughout the state Negroes were refusing to work on plantations for the miserable wages offered or on the sharecropping terms of semislavery. They wanted to be renters instead, and at fair rentals.

In the legislature, meanwhile, the Negro-white Republican majority was encouraging industry to come into the state, to modernize the economy and break the monopoly of the plant-

ers. To fill Jefferson Davis's seat in the United States Senate, they sent a Negro, Hiram R. Revels, to Washington.

The number of Negroes who were moving up the ladder to become shopowners, merchants, teachers, public officials, grew rapidly year by year. The 1873 election put sixty-four Negroes in the state legislature, and Negroes were chosen speaker of the house, lieutenant-governor, secretary of state, and superintendent of education. One of these, the former slave, Blanche K. Bruce, rose fast, from teacher to tax collector to sheriff to county superintendent of schools to the United States Senate, where he served the full six years.

In Mississippi, as in the other Southern states, the old rulers were determined to strangle the new society in its cradle. Whip and torch, hood and gun were taken up again in terror that rode the countryside unchecked. One local gang boasted they had killed one hundred sixteen Negroes and tossed their corpses into the Tallahatchie River. In one county, every Negro schoolhouse and church used as a school was burned down. In one year, over three hundred fifty arrests or indictments were made in the state by federal officials, but not one terrorist was punished. Negro leaders were being systematically slaughtered, and the Ku Klux Klan (led by General Albert Pike, the respected and famous explorer) seemed able to carry out its inquisition with impunity. One of its most hated targets was the militia unit, organized with federal sanction to provide some protection against terror. Although open to both races, the units were called the "Negro militia," and their leaders marked for destruction in "Dead Books."

Caldwell commanded a militia unit charged with keeping the peace in Clinton. In September, a month before the 1875 elections, he sought, unarmed, to stop whites from provoking a riot at the Republican parade and barbecue in Moss Hill. But firing broke out and both whites and Negroes were killed or wounded. For four days the village was the scene of a massacre of Negro and white radical leaders, with thirty-five to fifty killed by local whites and vigilantes called "Modocs" imported from Vicksburg.

How these events led up to Caldwell's murder is told in his wife's own words. She testified before a congressional committee chaired by Senator George Boutwell.

A notorious Negro . . .

1875

ABOUT FOUR O'CLOCK in the evening . . . he [her husband, Charles Caldwell] walked downtown a half hour, and came back and eat his dinner, and just between dark and sundown he goes back downtown again. He went downtown knocking about down there. I do not know what he was doing down there, until just nearly dusk, and a man, Madison Bell, a colored man, came and says, "Mrs. Caldwell you had better go down and see about Mr. Caldwell, I think the white folks will kill him; they are getting their guns and pistols, and you had better go and get your husband away from town."

I did not go myself; I did not want to go myself, but went to Professor Bell and said would he go and get him. Mr. Bell went, and he never came back at all until he came back under arrest.

I was at my room until just nearly dark.

The moon was quite young, and the chapel bell rang.

We live right by it. I knew the minute the bell tolled, what it all meant. And the young men that lived right across the street, when the bell tolled, they rushed right out; they went through the door and some slid down the window and over they sprang; some went over the fence. They all ran to the chapel and got their guns. There was 150 guns there to my own knowing; had been there since the riot, at the Baptist Chapel. They all got their guns.

I went downtown, and then all got ahead everywhere I went; and some of them wanted to know who I was, but I hid my face as well as I could. I just said "woman" and did not tell who I was.

As I got to town I went to go into Mr. Chilton's store and every store was closed just that quick, for it was early, about 6 o'clock. All the other stores were closed. Chilton's was lit by a big chandelier, and as I went over the lumber-yard I saw a dead man. I stumbled over him, and I looked at him, but I did not know who it was, and I went into Chilton's. As I put my foot up on the store steps, standing as close, maybe a few feet (everything was engaged in it that day), there was Judge [E. W.] Cabaniss, who was a particular friend of my husband; a particular friend to him. He was standing in the center with a gun with a blue strap, in the center of the jam; and as I went to go in they cussed me and threatened to hurt me, and "make it damned hot for me," and the judge among the balance; but he said he didn't know me afterward. And they all stood; nobody would let me go in; they all stood there with their guns.

I know there was two dead men there, but I did not think it was my husband at the time.

I stood right there, and as I stood there they said to me, "If you don't go away they would make it very damned hot for me"; and I did not say anything, and walked off, and walked right over the dead man. He was right in my path where I found the body. He was lying broadside on the street. I did not know who he was. I then stopped and tried to see who he was, and they were cursing at me to get out of the town, to get out.

Then I went up, and there was Mrs. Bates across the street, my next-door neighbor. I seed her little girl come up by us and she said, "Aunt Ann, did you see my uncle here?" I said, "I did not. I saw a dead body on the street. I did not know who he was." She said, "What in the world is going on downtown?" Says I, "I don't know, only killing people there." She says, "Aaron Bates's hand is shot all to pieces, and Dr. Bangs is killed." He was not killed, but was shot in the leg; nobody killed but my husband and brother.

I went over to the house, and went upstairs and back to my room and laid down a widow.

After I had been home I reckon three-quarters of an hour, nearly an hour, Parson Nelson came up—Preacher Nelson and he called me. I was away upstairs. He called several times, and says, "Answer, don't be afraid; nobody will hurt you." He says, "Don't be afraid; answer me"; and after I had made up my mind to answer, I answered him what he wanted, and he said, "I have come to tell you the news, and it is sad news to you. Nobody told me to come, but I come up to tell you." I didn't say anything. "Your husband is dead." He said, "He is killed, and your brother, too, Sam [her brother-in-law, Sam Caldwell]."

I never said anything for a good while. He told me nobody would hurt me then; and when I did speak, says I, "Mr. Nelson, why did they kill him?" He says, "I don't know anything about it." He said just those words, "I don't know anything about it." He says, after that, "Have you any men folks about the place?" I says, "No." He says: "You shan't be hurt; don't be afraid of us; you shan't be hurt."

I never said anything whatever. He went off.

Sam's wife was there at the same time with three little children. Of course it raised great excitement.

After a length of time, Professor Hillman, of the Institute, the young ladies' school or college, he brought the bodies to the house; brought up my husband, him and Frank Martin. Professor Hillman and Mr. Nelson had charge of the dead bodies, and they brought them to the house; and when they brought them, they carried them in the bedroom, both of them, and put them there; they seed to having them laid out, and fixed up, and all that.

Mr. Nelson said in my presence, I listed to him, he said, "A braver life never had died than Charley Caldwell. He never saw a man died with a manlier spirit in his life."

He told me he had brought him out of the cellar.

You see when they had shot Sam, his brother, it was him who was lying there on the street. They shot him right through his head, off his horse, when he was coming in from the country, and fell on the street. He was the man I stumbled over twice. I did not know who he was. When they shot him, they said they shot him for fear he would go out of town and bring in other people and raise a fuss. He found out, I suppose, that they had his brother in the cellar, so he just lay there dead; he that was never known to shoot a gun or pistol in his life—never knew how.

Mr. Nelson said that Buck Cabell carried him [Charles

Caldwell] into the cellar; persuaded him to go out and drink; insisted upon his taking a drink with him, and him and Buck Cabell never knowed anything against each other in his life; never had no hard words. My husband told him no, he didn't want any Christmas. He said, "You must take a drink with me" and entreated him, and said, "You must take a drink." He then took him by the arm and told him to drink for a Christmas treat; that he must drink, and carried him into Chilton's cellar, and they jingled the glasses, and at the tap of the glasses, and while each one held the glass, while they were taking the glasses, somebody shot right through the back from the outside of the gate window, and he fell to the ground.

As they struck their glasses, that was the signal to shoot. They had him in the cellar, and shot him right there, and he fell on the ground.

When he was first shot, he called for Judge Cabiniss, and called for Mr. Chilton; I don't know who else. They were all around, and nobody went to his relief; all of them men standing around with their guns. Nobody went to the cellar, and he called for Preacher Nelson, called for him, and Preacher Nelson said that when he went to the cellar door he was afraid to go in, and called to him two or three times, "Don't shoot me," and Charles said, "Come in" he wouldn't hurt him and "take me out of the cellar," that he wanted to die in the open air, and did not want to die like a dog closed up.

When they taken him out, he was in a manner dead, just from that one shot; and they brings him out then, and he only asked one question, so Parson Nelson told me—to take him home and let him see his wife before he died; that he could not live long.

It was only a few steps to my house, and they would not do it, and some said this.

Nelson carried him to the middle of the street, and the men all hallooed, "We will save him while we've got him; dead men tell no tales." Preacher Nelson told me so. That is what they all cried, "We'll save him while we got him; dead men tell no tales."

Whether he stood up right there in the street while they riddled him with thirty or forty of their loads, of course, I do not know, but they shot him all that many times when he was in a manner dead. All those balls went in him.

I understood that a young gentleman told that they shot him as he lay on the ground until they turned him over. He said so. I did not hear him.

Mr. Nelson said when he asked them to let him see me they told him no, and he then said, taking both sides of his coat and bringing them up so, he said, "Remember when you kill me you kill a gentleman and a brave man. Never say you killed a coward. I want you to remember it when I am gone." Nelson told me that, and he said that he never begged them, and that he never told them, but to see how a brave man could die.

They can find no cause; but some said they killed him because he carried the militia to Edwards, and they meant to kill him for that. The time the guns were sent there, he was Captain under Governor Ames, and they said they killed him for that; for obeying Governor Ames.

After the bodies were brought to my house, Professor Hillman and Martin all stayed until one o'clock, and then at one o'clock the train came from Vicksburg with the "Murdocs." They all marched up to my house and went into where the two dead bodies laid, and they cursed them, those dead bodies, there, and they danced and threw open the window, and sung all their songs, and challenged the dead body to get up and meet them, and they carried on there like a parcel of wild Indians over those dead bodies, these Vicksburg "Murdocs." Just one or two colored folks were sitting up in the room, and they carried on all that in my presence, danced and sung and done anything they could. Some said they even struck them; but I heard them curse and challenge them to get up and fight. The Vicksburg "Murdocs" done that that night. Then they said they could not stay any longer. . . .

As for any other cause I never knew—but only they intended to kill him because for carrying the militia to Edwards, for obeying Governor Ames, and that was all they had against him.

At the same time, when they had the Moss Hill riot, the day of the dinner in September, when they came over that day, they telegraphed for the Vicksburg "Murdocs" to come out, and they came out at dark, and when they did come, about fifty came out to my house that night; and they were breaking the locks open on doors and trunks; whenever they would find it closed they would break the locks. And they taken from the house what guns they could find, and plundered and robbed the house. The captain of the Vicksburg "Murdocs"—his name is Tinney.

O. What day was that?

A. The 4th day of September. They came out, and Tinney stayed there, and at daybreak they commenced to go, and he, among others, told me to tell my husband that the Clinton people sent for him to kill him, and he named them who they were to kill—all the leaders especially, and he says, "Tell him when I saw him"—he was gone that night; he fled to Jackson that evening with all the rest—"we are going to kill him if it is two years, or one year, or six; no difference; we are going to kill him anyhow. We have orders to kill him, and we are going to do it, because he belongs to the Republican party, and is a leader, he has got to die." He told me that; and that the southern people are going to have the South back to ourselves, and no damned northern people and no Republican party; and if your husband don't join us he has got to die. Tell him I said so. I told him what he said. I did not know Tinney at the time; and when I saw my husband enter, I told him, and he knew him from what I said, and he saw him afterward and told him what I said. He just said that he said it for devilment. They carried on there until the next morning, one crowd after another. I had two wounded men. I brought them off the Moss Hill battle-field, and these men treated me very cruelly, and threatened to kill them, but they did not happen to kill them.

Next morning, before sun up, they went to a house where there was an old black man, a feeble old man, named Bob Beasly, and they shot him all to pieces. And they went to Mr. Willis's and took out a man, named Gamaliel Brown, and shot him all to pieces. It was early in the morning; and they goes out to Sam Jackson's, president of the club and they shot him all to pieces. He hadn't even time to put on his clothes. And they went out to Alfred Hastings; Alfred saw them coming. And this was before sun up.

Q. This morning after the Clinton riot?

A. On the morning of the 5th, and they shot Alfred Hastings all to pieces, another man named Ben. Jackson, and then they goes out and shoots one or two further up on the Madison road; I don't know exactly; the name of one was Lewis Russell. He was shot, and Moses Hill. They were around that morning killing people before breakfast. I saw a young man from Vicksburg that I knew, and I asked him what it all meant.

Q. Who was he?

A. Dr. Hardesty's son; and I asked him what did it mean, their killing black people that day? He says, "You all had a big dinner yesterday, and paraded around with your drums and flags. That was impudence to the white people. You have no right to do it. You have got to leave these damned Negroes; leave them and come on to our side. You have got to join the Democratic party. We are going to kill all the Negroes. The Negro men shall not live."

And they didn't live; for every man they found they killed that morning, and did not allow any one to escape them, so he said. So he told me all they intended to do about the colored people for having their dinner and parading there, and having their banners; and intended to kill the white Republicans the same. Didn't intend to leave any one alive they could catch, and they did try to get hold of them, and went down on Monday morning to kill the school-teacher down there, Haffa, but he escaped. Jo Stevens and his son Albert Stevens, I believe, was his name—they just murdered them right on through. These people stayed there at the store and plundered it, and talked that they intended to kill them until they got satisfaction for three white people that was killed in that battle. I can show who was the first white man that started the riot; and I can show you I have got his coat and pants, and I can show you how they shot him. They blamed all on my husband, and I asked what they killed Sam for; asked Dr. Alexander. They said they killed him because they were afraid he would tell about killing his brother. They killed my husband for obeying Governor Ames's orders, and they cannot find anything he did. He didn't do anything to be killed for. . . .

From "Report of the Select Committee to Inquire into the Mississippi Election of 1875 . . . ," Report No. 527, 44th Congress, 1st Session, Vol. I (Serial No. 1669).

"You must make peace at any price." That was the message the Negro people got from the election of 1876. Its outcome marked the end of Reconstruction. In the early returns, the Democratic candidate backed by the South, Samuel J. Tilden, seemed to have defeated the Republican, Rutherford B. Hayes. But a complicated dispute rose over the last crucial electoral votes, and was settled in Hayes' favor by a bipartisan electoral commission. Behind the dubious victory of the Republicans and its acceptance by the Democrats was an elaborate and secret maneuver between spokesmen for the two candidates. The Republicans got the Presidency and the Democrats got a pledge to let the South have "home rule" and the economic aid it badly needed.

Hayes took office in March, 1877, and promptly withdrew the last federal troops from the South. The white Democrats were now in complete control of everything, including the constitutional rights Negroes might exercise. Hayes went South in September on a "good-will" tour. He would follow a hands-off policy, he said, counting on "the great mass of intelligent white men" to protect the Negroes' rights.

How much that faith was worth is reported in this editorial from a Negro newspaper. It showed that some Negroes would not rely on faith alone. When a Negro was lynched in Tennessee, the colored people set fire to the town.

A choice between blood and liberty . . .

1880

CLARKSVILLE, TENNESSEE, was
visited last week by a terrible fire. The business portion of the
town was burned, leaving a mere shell of suburban residence
in place of the great tobacco mart of Tennessee. It is supposed
to be the work of incendiaries and the colored people bear the
blame. When the city was burning, they gathered in little knots
and crowds; discussed the situation, witnessed with a good
deal of manifest satisfaction the strenuous effort to suppress
the fire, but would not lend a helping hand, for love or money.

We are loath to advocate lawlessness. We deplore the necessity of resorting to arson and rapine but if such things must
come, let them come. If the colored people of Clarksville did
fire the town, we regret the necessity but not the act. If they
have been denied the rights and privileges of men; if, by studied
persecution, their hearts have been hardened; if goaded by oppression to desperation they have lost all their interest in and
love for their homes; we are proud to see them have the manhood to be the willing witnesses of its destruction.

A CHOICE BETWEEN BLOOD AND LIBERTY

The colored people of Clarksville were incensed over a multitude of wrongs. Not long ago, a colored man was lynched upon the charge of an attempt at outrage. An attempt, mind you. This is a comprehensive term in the South. It embraces a wink by a colored man at a white girl a half mile off. Such a crime is worthy of lynching, but a beastly attack upon a colored girl by a white man is only a wayward indiscretion. The colored people have stood such discriminations long enough.

The people of Clarksville have broken the ice, God grant it may extend from Virginia to Texas. Still later, a colored man was brutally killed by a policeman, and ever since, the people have given forth mutterings, not loud, but deep. . . .

[President] Hayes has plainly told the colored people they must make peace at any price. We repeat it, but with a different signification—they must make peace at any price. It may cost treasure, it may cost blood, it may cost lives, but make it, be the cost what it may. . . .

The trying scenes of a presidential contest will soon be upon us. We claim no prophetic vision, but we warn the southern whites that they need not expect such one-sided scenes of butchery in future. They will have to make a choice between Blood, the Brand, and Political Liberty.

From Chicago *Conservator*, 1880.

All Colored People

THAT WANT TO

GO TO KANSAS,

On September 5th, 1877,

Can do so for $5.00

I n 1877, they lost all hope. The whole South, said one Negro leader, had got into the hands of the very men that had held them slaves. If they stayed where they were, under these men, they might as well be slaves. And so alone, in families, by hundreds and then by thousands they began to go north. It was an exodus like the Hebrew flight from slavery on the Nile.

Colored conventions in New Orleans and Nashville urged systematic and organized emigration of Negroes to parts of the country where they could enjoy all the rights granted by the Constitution and the laws. Southerners, alarmed by the loss of both plantation hands and skilled artisans, tried persuasion and then force to keep the Negro at home. Among Negro leaders a debate developed over the exodus. Frederick Douglass hoped the Negroes would give democracy a bit more time to take hold in the South, while Richard T. Greener, dean of Howard University's law school, said only the North and the

West would give the Negro a chance to show what he could do under freedom.

The "exodusters," as they were called, swarmed from even the deepest reaches of the South up into Kansas. Many met disaster there, for they came without money and shivered and starved on the bleak plains.

Some Kansans welcomed the immigrants, but others tore down or burned their rude barracks. Their plight reached the outside world and relief societies formed to send assistance. Many of the exodusters stopped in states along the way or settled in Chicago. But few, whether they prospered or not, ever thought of going back South.

When the wave of immigration rose higher and higher, the United States Senate decided to investigate it. The Democrats said the movement was only a Republican plot to swell the party rolls in the Midwest, and that greedy rail and shipping companies were encouraging it to get the business.

The true story came from the lips of Henry Adams, a witness before the committee. He was an illiterate Negro, a veteran of the Union Army, and he had taken a leading part in the great migration.

Exodus ...

1880

Q. Now TELL US, Mr. Adams, what, if anything, you know about the exodus of the colored people from the Southern to the Northern and Western States; and be good enough to tell us in the first place what you know about the organization of any committee or society among the colored people themselves for the purpose of bettering their condition, and why it was organized. Just give us a history of that as you understand it.

A. I went into the Army in 1866 and came out the last of 1869—and went right back home again where I went from, Shreveport. . . . After we have come out a parcel of we men that was in the Army and other men thought that the way our people had been treated during the time we was in service— we heard so much talk of how they had been treated and opposed so much and there was no help for it. That caused me to go into the Army at first, the way our people was opposed. There was so much going on that I went off and left it; when

96

I came back it was still going on, part of it, not quite so bad as at first. So a parcel of us got together and said that we would organize ourselves into a committee and look into affairs and see the true condition of our race, to see whether it it was possible we could stay under a people who had held us under bondage. . . . We organized a committee.

Q. What did you call your committee?

A. We just called it a committee. . . . Some of the members of the committee was ordered by the committee to go into every State in the South where we had been slaves there, and post one another from time to time about the true condition of our race, and nothing but the truth.

Q. I want to know how many traveled in that way to get at the condition of your people in the Southern States?

A. I think about one hundred or one hundred and fifty went from one place or another.

Q. And they went from one place to another, working their way and paying their expenses and reporting to the common center at Shreveport, do you mean?

A. Yes, sir.

Q. What was the character of the information that they gave you?

A. . . . they said in several parts where they was that the land rent was still higher there in that part of the country than it was where we first organized it, and the people was still being whipped, some of them, by the old owners, the men that had owned them as slaves, and some of them was being cheated out of their crops just the same as they was there.

Q. Was anything said about their personal and political rights in these reports, as to how they were treated about these?

A. Yes, some of them stated that in some parts of the country where they voted they would be shot. Some of them stated that if they voted the Democratic ticket they would not be injured.

Q. But that they would be shot, or might be shot, if they voted the Republican ticket?

A. Yes, sir.

Q. I am speaking now of the period from 1870 to 1874, and you have given us the general character of the reports that you got from the South; what did you do in 1874?

A. Well, along in August sometime in 1874, after the white league sprung up, they organized and said this is a white man's government, and the colored men should not hold any offices; they were no good but to work in the fields and take what they would give them and vote the Democratic ticket. That's what they would make public speeches and say to us, and we would hear them. We then organized an organization called the colonization council.

Q. What was the difference between that organization and your committee, as to its objects?

A. Well, the committee was to investigate the condition of our race.

Q. And this organization was then to better your condition after you had found out what that condition was?

A. Yes, sir.

Q. In what way did you propose to do it?

A. We first organized and adopted a plan to appeal to the President of the United States and to Congress to help us out of our distress, or protect us in our rights and privileges.

Q. Well, what other plan had you?

A. And if that plan failed our idea was then to ask them to set apart a territory in the United States for us, somewhere where we could go and live with our families.

Q. You preferred to go off somewhere by yourselves?

A. Yes.

Q. Well, what then?

A. If that failed, our other object was to ask for an appropriation of money to ship us all to Liberia, in Africa; somewhere where we could live in peace and quiet.

Q. Yes, and what after that?

A. When that failed then our idea was to appeal to other governments outside of the United States to help us get away from the United States and go there and live under their flag.

Q. Now when you organized the council what kind of people were taken into it?

A. Nobody but laboring men. . . . When we met in committee there was not any of us allowed to tell our name. . . . We first appealed to President Grant. . . . That was in September, 1874 . . . at other times we sent to Congress. . . . We told them our condition, and asked Congress to help us out of our distress and protect us in our lives and property, and pass some law or provide some way that we might get our rights in the South, and so forth. . . . After the appeal in 1874, we appealed when the time got so hot down there they stopped our churches from having meetings after nine o'clock at night. They stopped them from sitting up and singing over the dead, and so forth, right in the little town where we lived, in Shreveport. I know that to be a fact; and after they did all this, and we saw it was getting so warm—killing our people all over the whole country—there was several of them killed right down in our parish—we appealed. . . .

We had much rather stayed there [in the South] if we could have had our rights. . . . In 1877 we lost all hopes . . . we found ourselves in such condition that we looked around and we seed that there was no way on earth, it seemed, that we could better our condition there, and we discussed that thoroughly in our organization along in May. We said that the whole South—every State in the South—had got into the hands of the very men that held us slaves—from one thing to another and we thought that the men that held us slaves was holding the reins of government over our heads in every respect almost, even the constable up to the governor. We felt we had almost as well be slaves under these men. . . .

We said there was no hope for us and we had better go. . . . Then, in 1877 we appealed to President Hayes and to Congress, to both Houses. I am certain we sent papers there; if they didn't get them that is not our fault; we sent them. . . .

Mighty few ministers would allow us to have their churches [for meetings]; some few would in some of the parishes. . . . When we held our meetings we would not allow the politicians to speak. . . .

It is not exactly five hundred men belonging to the council . . . they have now got at this time 98,000 names enrolled . . . men and women, and none under twelve years old . . . some in Louisiana—the majority of them in Louisiana, and some in Texas, and some in Arkansas . . . a few in Mississippi . . . a few in Alabama [and] in a great many of the others. . . .

Q. Now, Mr. Adams, you know, probably, more about the

causes of the exodus from that country than any other man, from your connection with it; tell us in a few words what you believe to be the causes of these people going away?

A. Well, the cause is, in my judgment, and from what information I have received, and what I have seen with my own eyes—it is because the largest majority of the people, of the white people, that held us as slaves treats our people so bad in many respects that it is impossible for them to stand it. Now, in a great many parts of that country there our people most as well be slaves as to be free; because, in the first place, I will state this: that in some times, in times of politics, if they have any idea that the Republicans will carry a parish or ward, or something of that kind, why, they would do anything on God's earth. There ain't nothing too mean for them to do to prevent it; nothing I can make mention of is too mean for them to do. . . .

From Senate Report No. 693, 46th Congress, 2nd Session, part 2.

BOOKER T. WASHINGTON

T*he anaconda is a large snake which crushes its prey. To Louisiana novelist George W. Cable, his own South had become "a land of long hours, low wages and anaconda mortgages." It was the late 1880's, and he was writing about the cotton states which had become merely a tax-payers' government devoted to protecting the right of landholders and storekeepers to crush the Negro and white farm tenants.*

Cable, a former Confederate cavalry officer, was a little man, gentle and scholarly. He and his friend Mark Twain were the first major Southern writers to portray the Negro sympathetically in their fiction. He had come to hate the color-caste system and began writing articles in national magazines, exposing the convict labor system, arguing for prison reform, pleading for equity and social justice. He appealed especially to the "silent South"—the many Southerners who wished racism would disappear but were too scared to speak their convictions.

In 1884 Cable left the South, settling in Northampton, Massachusetts. He was the friend of many Negroes, including W. E. B. DuBois and Booker T. Washington, who visited him at his home. But even here, in the liberal town where Washington's daughter was attending Smith College, restaurants refused to serve Cable's friends, and Cable was censured for inviting them to his table.

To gather material for one of his articles, Cable asked Washington for facts on how the tenant farming system worked. Washington, who had started Tuskegee Institute in 1881, in the heart of the black belt, knew the problem thoroughly and sent this reply.

The anaconda . . .
1889

WHEN THE WAR ENDED the colored people had nothing on which to live while the first crop was being made. Thus, in addition to renting the land on which to make the first crop they had to get the local merchant or someone else to supply the food for the family to eat while the first crop was being made. For every dollar's worth of provisions so advanced the local merchant charged from 12 to 30 per cent interest. In order to be sure that he secured his principal and interest a mortgage or lien was taken on the crop, in most cases not then planted.

Of course the farmers could pay no such interest and the end of the first year found them in debt—the 2nd year they tried again, but there was the old debt and the new interest to pay, and in this way the "mortgage system" has gotten a hold on everything that it seems impossible to shake off. Its evils have grown instead of decreasing, until it is safe to say that ⅚ of the colored farmers mortgage their crops every year.

Not only their crops before, in many cases, they are actually planted, but their wives sign a release from the homestead law and in most every case mules, cows, wagons, plows and often all household furniture is covered by the lien.

At a glance one is not likely to get the full force of the figures representing the amount of interest charged. Example, if a man makes a mortgage with a merchant for $200 on which to "run" during the year the farmer is likely to get about $50 of this amount in February or March, $50 May, $50 in June or July and the remainder in Aug. or Sept. By the middle of Sept. the farmer begins returning the money in cotton and by the last of Oct. whatever he can pay the farmer has paid, but the merchant charges as much for the money gotten in July or Aug. as for that gotten in Feb. The farmer is charged interest on all for the one year of 12 months. And as the "advance" is made in most cases in provisions rather than cash, the farmer, in addition to paying the interest mentioned, is charged more for the same goods than one buying for cash. If a farmer has 6 in a family, say wife and 4 children, the merchant has it in his power to feed only those who work and sometimes he says to the farmer if he sends his children to school no rations can be drawn for them while they are attending school.

After a merchant has "run" a farmer for 5 or 6 years and he does not "pay out" or decides to try mortgaging with another merchant the first merchant in such cases usually "cleans up" the farmer, that is takes everything, mules, cows, plows, chicken's fodder—everything except wife and children.

It is not very often that the merchant furnishing the supplies owns the land, this in most cases is rented from a different party. So you see that the 2 parties, farmer and merchant, who have the most contact with the land, have no interest in it except to get all they can out of it.

The result of all this is seen in the "general run down" condition of ⅘ of the farms in Alabama—houses unpainted—fences tumbling down, animals poorly cared for, and the land growing poorer every year. Many of the colored farmers have almost given up hope and do just enough work to secure their "advances." One of the strongest things that can be said in favor of the colored people is, that in almost every community there are one or two who have shaken off this yoke of slavery and have bought farms of their own and are making money—and there are a few who rent land and "mortgage" and still do something.

The practices that I have referred to are in most cases sanctioned by the laws of the legislature and are not prohibited by law. . . .

From *The Journal of Negro Education,* 1948, XVII.

The Panic of 1873 had been a
disaster for America's farmers, and thousands lost their land.
They were squeezed hard and dry by the banks, the railroads,
and the farm machinery manufacturers, and if anything at all
was left, taxes took it away.

The hungry farmers, believing that both major parties were
the tools of big business, organized into the Southern Farmers'
Alliance. It experimented with cooperative buying and selling,
as well as social and educational programs. But when it became clear that it would not take in Negroes, a Colored Farmers' Alliance grew up parallel to it and by 1891 claimed more
than a million members. The two groups cooperated more and
more. In Georgia, the white radical leader, Tom Watson,
urged Negro and white to join together to put down the mon-
eyed interests who were fleecing them all.

Out of that spirit came a coalition between the Populist Party and the Republicans which tried to win Negro support in most Southern states and fought alongside the Negro to secure his franchise. It called for reforms in land, transportation, taxes, and other policies. In some states—especially Georgia and North Carolina—progress was made and Negroes won local and state offices. In others, redistricting, fraud, and violence were used by the Democrats to beat back the threat to their power. Sometimes the very Democrats who had driven the Negro from the polls just a few short years before, now tried to buy or coerce his support.

But the agrarian revolt collapsed before the end of the Nineties. The old conservatives shouted "Negro domination" again and the poor and ignorant white farmers were turned back into their old racist ways. The Populist reform measures would have helped both Negro and white, but the color line drawn between them defeated both. The radical leaders such as Tom Watson and Ben Tillman hopped onto the Democratic Party again and became ranting demagogues. Now they denied the Negro's right to take part in politics and led the South into widespread adoption of laws disfranchising the Negro and segregating him in every walk of life.

In Florida, the Rev. J. L. Moore, a county leader of the Colored Farmers' Alliance, wrote a letter to a Washington publication telling how his group felt about the common bond between black and white who worked for a living. Unfortunately, his hopes were not realized for very long.

We join hands . . .
1891

AS MEMBERS of the Colored
Farmers' Alliance we avowed that we were going to vote with
and for the man or party that will secure for the farmer or
laboring man his just rights and privileges, and in order that
he may enjoy them without experiencing a burden.

We want protection at the ballot box, so that the laboring
man may have an equal showing, and the various labor organizations to secure their just rights, we will join hands with them
irrespective of party. . . . We are aware of the fact that the
laboring colored man's interests and the laboring white man's
interests are one and the same. Especially is this true at the
South. Anything that can be brought about to benefit the
workingman, will also benefit the Negro more than any other
legislation that can be enacted. . . . So I for one have fully
decided to vote with and work for that party, or those who
favor the workingman, let them belong to the Democratic,
or Republican, or the People's Party. I know I speak the sen-

timent of that convention, representing as we do one-fifth of the laborers of this country, seven-eights of our race in this country being engaged in agricultural pursuits.

Can you wonder why we have turned our attention from the few pitiful offices a few of our members could secure, and turned our attention toward benefiting the mass of our race, and why we are willing to legislate that this mass be benefited? And we ask Congress to protect the ballot box, so they may be justly dealt with in their effort to gain that power. We know and you know that neither of the now existing parties is going to legislate in the interest of the farmers or laboring men except so far as it does not conflict with their interest to do so. . . .

Can we do anything while the present parties have control of the ballot box, and we [the Alliance] have no protection? The greatest mistake, I see, is this: The wily politicians see and know that they have to do something, therefore they are slipping into the Alliance, and the farmers, in many instances, are accepting them as leaders; and if we are to have the same leaders, we need not expect anything else but the same results. The action of the Alliance in this reminds me of the man who first put his hand in the lion's mouth and the lion finally bit it off; and then he changed to make the matter better and put his head in the lion's mouth, and therefore lost his head. Now the farmers and laboring men know in the manner they were standing before they organized; they lost their hands, so to speak; now organized in one body or head, if they give themselves over to the same power that took their hand, it will likewise take their head.

Now, Mr. Editor, I wish to say, if the laboring men of the

United States will lay down party issues and combine to enact laws for the benefit of the laboring man, I, as county superintendent of Putnam County Colored Farmers' Alliance, and member of the National Colored Farmers, know that I voice the sentiment of that body, representing as we did 750,000 votes, when I say we are willing and ready to lay down the past, take hold with them irrespective of party, race, or creed, until the cry shall be heard from the Heights of Abraham of the North, to the Everglades of Florida, and from the rock-bound coast of the East, to the Golden Eldorado of the West, that we can heartily endorse the motto, "Equal rights to all and special privileges to none."

From *The National Economist,* March 7, 1891.

Frederick Douglass

I*n 1882 the Tuskegee Institute begun to keep records of the lynchings in the United States. Until the end of the century the number never fell below one hundred for any one year, and often it would rise far above. In 1884—211; in 1892—235; in 1893—200. By 1900 the grand total was 3,011 Negroes shot, hung, burned, beaten, or tortured to death. The first bill to make lynching a federal crime was introduced by George H. White of North Carolina, the last Negro to sit in Congress during the post-Reconstruction period.*

The most common charge made by the lynch mobs against their victims was rape of a white woman. To it Frederick Douglass made this reply in 1892.

Excuse for lynching . . .

1892

THE CRIME which these usurpers of courts of law and juries profess to punish is the most revolting and shocking of any this side of murder. This they know is the best excuse, and it appeals at once and promptly to a prejudice which prevails at the North as well as the South. Hence we have for any act of lawless violence the same excuse —an outrage by a Negro upon some white woman. It is a notable fact, also, that it is not with them the immorality or the enormity of the crime itself that arouses popular wrath, but the emphasis is put upon the race and color of the parties to it. Here, and not there, is the ground of indignation and abhorrence. The appeal is not to the moral sense but to the well-known hatred of one class to another. . . .

For 200 years or more white men have in the South committed this offense against black women, and the fact has excited little attention, even at the North, except among Abolitionists; which circumstance demonstrates that the horror now excited is not for the crime itself, but that it is based on the reversal of color in the participants. . . .

Now where rests the responsibility for the lynch law prevalent in the South? It is evident that it is not entirely with the ignorant mob. The men who break open jails and with bloody hands destroy human life are not alone responsible. These are not the men who make public sentiment. They are simply the hangmen, not the court, judge, or jury. They simply obey the public sentiment of the South—the sentiment created by wealth and respectability, by the press and pulpit. A change in public sentiment can be easily effected by these forces whenever they shall elect to make the effort. Let the press and the pulpit of the South unite their power against the cruelty, disgrace and shame that is settling like a mantle of fire upon these lynch-law States, and lynch law itself will soon cease to exist.

Nor is the South alone responsible for this burning shame and menace to our free institutions. Wherever contempt of race prevails, whether against African, Indian or Mongolian, countenance and support are given to the present peculiar treatment of the Negro in the South. The finger of scorn at the North is correlated to the dagger of the assassin at the South. The sin against the Negro is both sectional and national; and until the voice of the North shall be heard in emphatic condemnation and withering reproach against these continued ruthless mob law murders, it will remain equally involved with the South in this common crime.

From *Christian Recorder*, August 11, 1892.

STUDENTS OF FORESTRY AT BOOKER T. WASHINGTON'S
TUSKEGEE INSTITUTE

The abilities Booker T. Washington had shown at Hampton Institute, the first successful agricultural and industrial school for Negroes, won for him the post of principal of the new Negro school founded at Tuskegee in 1881. The Institute started with almost nothing, and was built into a large and flourishing school by the leadership of Washington and the labors of the students. With their own bricks they built the workshops where they were trained to be carpenters, blacksmiths, printers, shoemakers. Work was no disgrace, but an honor, Washington preached. The Negro must start where slavery left him, at the bottom, and work his way up to equality with the whites. Tuskegee taught Negro farmers how to get the most out of their land and Negro businessmen how to organize for their mutual benefit.

This emphasis on industrial and agricultural education for the Negro was not new, of course. Schools for manual labor and the domestic sciences had been advocated for the past sixty years. To overcome barriers raised against Negro progress by white employers and workers, Frederick Douglass and the Negro conventions had argued that a policy of self-help and trade schools would make Negroes valuable to society and win its respect. Most of the early Negro schools fostered programs of industrial education whose theme was help yourself—with white guidance—and you will acquire property and high moral standards. Along the road, somewhere in the dim future, the blessings of full citizenship will be bestowed upon you.

The "uplift" program had a natural appeal for whites both North and South. It expressed the Yankee virtues of hard work and individual initiative and promised to provide a trained and docile labor supply. And since it accepted an inferior position for the Negro in the long period while he would be straining to lift himself up by his bootstraps, it pleased the Southern whites, too.

At Tuskegee, Washington assured white neighbors that the school was there to serve the community. Gradually he overcame their suspicion by providing the services and the produce that they needed. He won the support of white leaders by counselling the Negroes to obey the laws and keep the peace. Northern philanthropists gave large sums to Tuskegee, and Southern politicians, who had feared education would "ruin our Negroes," relaxed when they heard no demands for equality.

At the Cotton States Exposition in Atlanta in 1895, Washington was invited to make a speech. It was an unusual honor to be tendered by whites. Still, there was only polite handclapping when he was introduced. But when Washington finished, the ovation signalled the fact that the policy he voiced would overnight make him the most famous Negro in the country and the most influential among powerful whites.

Cast down your bucket where you are . . .

1895

A SHIP LOST AT SEA for many days suddenly sighted a friendly vessel. From the mast of the unfortunate vessel was seen the signal: "Water, water, we die of thirst." The answer from the friendly vessel at once came back, "Cast down your bucket where you are." A second time the signal, "Water, water, send us water," ran up from the distressed vessel and was answered, "Cast down your bucket where you are," and a third and fourth signal for water was answered "Cast down your bucket where you are." The captain of the distressed vessel, at last heeding the injunction, cast down his bucket and it came up full of fresh, sparkling water from the mouth of the Amazon River. To those of my race who depend on bettering their condition in a foreign land, or who underestimate the importance of cultivating friendly relations with the Southern white man who is their next door neighbor, I would say, cast down your bucket where you are, cast it down in making friends, in every manly way, of the people of all races by whom you are surrounded. Cast it down in agriculture, in mechanics, in commerce, in domestic service, and in the professions. And in this connection it is well to bear in mind that, whatever other sins the South may be called upon to bear, when it comes to business pure and simple it is in the South that the Negro is given a man's chance in the commercial world; and in nothing is this Exposition more eloquent than in emphasizing this chance. Our greatest danger is, that, in the great leap from slavery to freedom, we may overlook the fact that the masses of us are to live by the productions of our hands, and fail to keep in mind that we shall prosper in the proportion as we learn to dignify and glorify common labor and put brains and skill into the common occupations of life; shall prosper in proportion as we learn to draw the line between the superficial and the substantial, the ornamental gewgaws of life and the useful. No race can prosper till it learns that there is as much dignity in tilling a field as in writing a poem. It is at the bottom of life we must begin and not the top. Nor should we permit our grievances to overshadow our opportunities.

To those of the white race who look to the incoming of those of foreign birth and strange tongue and habits for the prosperity of the South, were I permitted, I would repeat what I say to my own race, "Cast down your bucket where you are." Cast it down among the 8,000,000 Negroes whose habits you know, whose loyalty and love you have tested in days when to have proved treacherous meant the ruin of your firesides. Cast it down among those people who have, without strikes and labor wars, tilled your fields, cleared your forests, built your railroads and cities, and brought forth treasures from the bowels of the earth and helped make possible this magnificent representation of the progress of the South. Casting down your bucket among my people, helping and encouraging as you are doing on these grounds, and with education of head, hand and heart, you will find that they will buy your surplus land, make blossom the waste places in your fields, and run your factories. While doing this you can be sure in the future, as you have been in the past, that you and your families will be surrounded by the most patient, faithful, law-abiding, and unresentful people that the world has seen. As we have proved our loyalty to you in the past, in nursing your children, watching by the sick beds of your mothers and fathers, and often following them with tear-dimmed eyes to their graves, so in the future, in our humble way, we shall stand by you with a devotion that no foreigner can approach, ready to lay down our lives, if need be, in defense of yours; interlacing our industrial, commercial, civil, and religious life with yours in a way that shall make the interests of both races one. In all things that are purely social we can be as separate as the fingers, yet one as the hand in all things essential to mutual progress.

There is no defense or security for any of us except in the highest intelligence and development of all. If anywhere there are efforts tending to curtail the fullest growth of the Negro, let these efforts be turned into stimulating, encouraging and making him the most useful and intelligent citizen. Effort or means so invested will pay a thousand per cent interest. These efforts will be twice blessed—"blessing him that gives and him that takes."

There is no escape, through law of man or God, from the inevitable:

"The laws of changeless justice bind
Oppressor with oppressed,
And close as sin and suffering joined
We march to fate abreast."

Nearly sixteen millions of hands will aid you pulling the load upwards, or they will pull against you the load downwards. We shall constitute one-third and much more of the ignorance and crime of the South, or one-third its intelligence and progress; we shall contribute one-third to the business and industrial prosperity of the South, or we shall prove a veritable body of death, stagnating, depressing, retarding every effort to advance the body politic.

The wisest among my race understand that the agitation of questions of social equality is the extremest folly, and the progress in the enjoyment of all the privileges that will come to us must be the result of severe and constant struggle, rather than of artificial forcing. No race that has anything to contribute to the markets of the world is long in any degree ostracized. It is important that we be prepared for the exercise of these privileges. The opportunity to earn a dollar in a factory just now is worth infinitely more than the opportunity to spend a dollar in an opera house.

In conclusion, may I repeat, that nothing in thirty years has given us more hope and encouragement and drawn us so near to you of the white race as the opportunity offered by this Exposition; here bending, as it were, over the altar that represents the results of the struggles of your race and mine, both starting practically empty-handed three decades ago, I pledge that, in your effort to work out the great and intricate problem which God has laid at the doors of the South, you shall have at all times the patient, sympathetic help of my race. Only let this be constantly in mind, that while, from representations in these buildings of the products of field, of forest, of mine, of factory, letters and art, much good will come—yet, far above and beyond material benefit, will be that higher good, that let us pray God will come, in a blotting out of sectional differences and racial animosities and suspicions, and in a determination, even in the remotest corner, to administer absolute justice; in a willing obedience among all classes to the mandates of law, and a spirit that will tolerate nothing but the highest equity in the enforcement of law. This, this, coupled with material prosperity, will bring into our beloved South new heaven and new earth.

From Alice M. Bacon, *The Negro and the Atlanta Exposition*, 1896.

JOHN HOPE

*B*ooker T. Washington's "At-
lanta Compromise" speech, as it came to be known, was hailed
nationally as the formula for peace between the races. For
many whites it put the Negro nicely in his "place." They took
Washington's program of expediency as the final solution to
the Negro problem and treated him as the spokesman for the
millions of his people.

But there were other Negro leaders who differed with Washington. The foremost spokesman of the previous generation,
the militant Frederick Douglass, had died a few months before the Atlanta speech. Now others were coming up. Among
them was John Hope. Born in Georgia in 1868, he worked
his way through Worcester Academy and Brown University.

Washington then invited him to teach at Tuskegee, but young as Hope was, he knew he was on a different path. Instead, he took a post in Nashville at Roger Williams University, a liberal arts college for Negroes. When he heard that Washington was to speak at Atlanta, he made it a point to go down and hear him. He thought deeply about the implications of Washington's speech, and on February 22 of the next year, speaking to the colored debating society of Nashville, he challenged Washington's "compromise."

Only twenty-eight then, Hope was making a brilliant record as a teacher, and within a few years was asked to come to Atlanta Baptist College to teach the classics. "Going back to Georgia, when for your race Georgia is hell?" his friends asked. And he replied, "It may be hell, but my people are there, and I'm going home." Later, Hope was to become the first Negro president of the college. Because he was a leader of the anti-Bookerite movement, the philanthropists who followed Washington's advice shut off all funds to Hope's school in retaliation for his independence.

*I want equality—
nothing less . . .*

1896

IF WE ARE NOT striving for equality, in heaven's name for what are we living? I regard it as cowardly and dishonest for any of our colored men to tell white people or colored people that we are not struggling for equality. If money, education, and honesty will not bring to me as much privilege, as much equality as they bring to any American citizen, then they are to me a curse, and not a blessing. God forbid that we should get the implements with which to fashion our freedom, and then be too lazy or pusillanimous to fashion it. Let us not fool ourselves nor be fooled by others. If we cannot do what other freemen do, then we are not free. Yes, my friends, I want equality. Nothing less. I want all that my God-given powers will enable me to get, then why not equality? Now, catch your breath, for I am going to use an adjective: I am going to say we demand social equality. In this Republic we shall be less than freemen, if we have a whit less than that which thrift, education, and honor afford other freemen. If equality, political, economic, and social, is the boon of other men in this great country of ours, then equality, political, economic, and social, is what we demand. Why build a wall to keep me out? I am no wild beast, nor am I an unclean thing.

Rise, Brothers! Come let us possess this land. Never say: "Let well enough alone." Cease to console yourselves with adages that numb the moral sense. Be discontented. Be dissatisfied. "Sweat and grunt" under present conditions. Be as restless as the tempestuous billows on the boundless sea. Let your discontent break mountain-high against the wall of prejudice, and swamp it to the very foundation. Then we shall not have to plead for justice nor on bended knee crave mercy; for we shall be men. Then and not until then will liberty in its highest sense be the boast of our Republic.

From *The Story of John Hope,* by Ridgely Torrence, Macmillan, 1948.

By 1900 the myth of white supremacy had gripped the national mind. The belief that the darker races were naturally inferior was spread everywhere by the press. Even the most respected newspapers and literary magazines—from The New York Times to Harper's—were guilty of the crudest racism. The press played up crimes in which Negroes were involved, creating the stereotype of the criminal Negro. Poems, stories, articles, novels, editorials, cartoons, jokes by the thousand sketched the Negro as dull, stupid, ignorant, vicious, lazy; he was the clown, the thief, the liar. There was no attempt to be consistent, for in one "romance" the Negro was the faithful plantation hand ready to die for ol' Massa and in the next he was the degraded brute bent on ravishing ol' Missy behind the magnolias.

The superiority of the Anglo-Saxon was universally declaimed. Darwin's theories were twisted to prove that the white, and especially the Anglo-Saxon, was the fittest, destined to rule the colored. It was white America's task to spread its superiority over the earth. It became very easy for white Americans, who were used to imposing their will on the Negro, to take over Cuba and the Philippines and look farther abroad to see what other darker-skinned people were waiting to be civilized. America, by the end of the century, had convinced itself that it was unselfishly ready to shoulder the "White Man's Burden."

In a letter to a national magazine in 1902, one Negro mother tried to show how little whites knew of the Negro's life, and what the effect was.

A happy set of people . . .

1902

I AM A COLORED WOMAN, wife and mother. I have lived all my life in the South, and have often thought what a peculiar fact it is that the more ignorant the Southern whites are of us the more vehement they are in their denunciation of us. They boast that they have little intercourse with us, never see us in our homes, churches or places of amusement, but still they know us thoroughly.

They also admit that they know us in no capacity except as servants yet they say we are at our best in that single capacity. What philosophers they are! The Southerners say we Negroes are a happy, laughing set of people, with no thought of tomorrow. How mistaken they are! The educated, thinking Negro is just the opposite. There is a feeling of unrest, insecurity, almost panic among the best class of Negroes in the South. In our homes, in our churches, wherever two or three are gathered together, there is a discussion of what is best to do. Must we remain in the South or go elsewhere? Where can we go to feel that security which other people feel? Is it best to go in great numbers or only several families? These and many other things are discussed over and over. . . .

I know of houses occupied by poor Negroes in which a respectable farmer would not keep his cattle. It is impossible for them to rent elsewhere. All Southern real estate agents have "white property" and "colored property." In one of the largest Southern cities there is a colored minister, a graduate of Harvard, whose wife is an educated, Christian woman, who lived for weeks in a tumble-down rookery because he could neither rent nor buy in a respectable locality.

Many colored women, who wash, iron, scrub, cook or sew all the week to help pay the rent for these miserable hovels and help fill the many small mouths, would deny themselves some of the necessaries of life if they could take their little children and teething babies on the cars to the parks of a Sunday afternoon and sit under the trees, enjoy the cool breezes and breathe God's pure air for only two or three hours; but this is denied them. Some of the parks have signs, "No Negroes allowed on these grounds except as servants." Pitiful, pitiful customs and laws that make war on women and babes! There is no wonder that we die; the wonder is that we persist in living.

Fourteen years ago I had just married. My husband had saved sufficient money to buy a small home. On account of our limited means we went to the suburbs, on unpaved streets, to look for a home, only asking for a high, healthy locality. Some real estate agents were "sorry, but had nothing to suit," some had "just the thing," but we discovered on investigation that they had "just the thing" for an unhealthy pigsty. Others had no "colored property." One agent said that he had what we wanted, but we should have to go to see the lot after dark, or walk by and give the place a casual look; for, he said, "all the white people in the neighborhood would be down on me." Finally we bought this lot. When the house was being built we went to see it. Consternation reigned. We had ruined this neighborhood of poor people; poor as we, poorer in manners at least. The people who lived next door received the sympathy of their friends. When we walked on the street (there were no sidewalks) we were embarrassed by the stare of many unfriendly eyes.

Two years passed before a single woman spoke to me, and only then because I helped one of them when a little sudden trouble came to her. Such was the reception I, a happy young woman, just married, received from people among whom I wanted to make a home. Fourteen years have now passed, four children have been born to us, and one has died in this same home, among these same neighbors. Although the neighbors speak to us, and occasionally one will send a child to borrow the morning's paper or ask the loan of a pattern, not one woman has ever been inside of my house, not even at the times when a woman would doubly appreciate the slightest attention of a neighbor.

The Southerner boasts that he is our friend; he educates our children, he pays us for work and is most noble and generous to us. Did not the Negro by his labor for over three hundred years help to educate the white man's children? Is thirty equal to three hundred? Does a white man deserve praise for paying a black man for his work?

The Southerner also claims that the Negro gets justice. Not long ago a Negro man was cursed and struck in the face by an electric car conductor. The Negro knocked the conductor down and although it was clearly proven in a court of "justice" that the conductor was in the wrong the Negro had to pay a fine of $10. The judge told him "I fine you that much to teach you that you must respect white folks." The conductor was acquitted. "Most noble judge! A second Daniel!" This is the South's idea of justice. . . .

Whenever a crime is committed, in the South the policemen look for the Negro in the case. A white man with face and hands blackened can commit any crime in the calendar. The first friendly stream soon washes away his guilt and he is ready to join in the hunt to lynch the "big, black burly brute." When a white man in the South does commit a crime, that is simply one white man gone wrong. If his crime is especially brutal he is a freak or temporarily insane. If one low, ignorant black wretch commits a crime, that is different. All of us must bear his guilt. A young white boy's badness is simply the overflowing of young animal spirits; the black boy's badness is badness, pure and simple. . . .

Someone will at last arise who will champion our cause and compel the world to see that we deserve justice; as other heroes compelled it to see that we deserved freedom.

From *The Independent,* September 18, 1902.

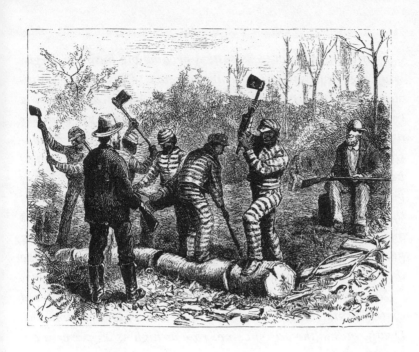

T*he   Reconstruction   regimes*
were often attacked for the taxes they levied to pay the costs of
their progressive programs. When the white conservatives got
into power, they protected their own purses by cutting the tax
burden. The way they handled the state penitentiary systems
showed they not only knew how to save themselves money, but
how to make it. They leased the convicts to private corpora-
tions or individuals. It was very profitable, for the state saved
on the maintenance of the prisoners while it took in revenue
from the sale of their forced labor.

Swiftly the convict-lease system became big business. Legislatures gave leases of ten to thirty years to prominent politicians. One Georgia senator held three hundred men on a twenty-year lease to mine his coal for eight cents per man per day. The great Tennessee Coal and Iron Company took all that state's prisoners for $101,000 a year. Of course the profits to be made at both ends led cooperative judges to inflict heavy penalties for petty offenses. And the Negro, now defenseless in the courts, was railroaded into the jails on his way to forests and swamps and plantations and mines where he was usually pent up like an animal in rolling cages. His life was much like that of the concentration camp prisoner of Hitler Germany.

Northern and Southern businessmen alike built fortunes out of the brutal labor and the shortened lives of the convicts. Death rates in the prison camps rose as high as 25 per cent annually.

A Negro in Georgia, hired out to work on a farm at the age of ten, tells the story of thirty years in peonage, working side by side with convict labor.

Hell itself . . .

1905

I AM A NEGRO and was born sometime during the war in Elbert County, Ga., and I reckon by this time I must be a little over forty years old. My mother was not married when I was born, and I never knew who my father was or anything about him. Shortly after the war my mother died, and I was left to the care of my uncle. All this happened before I was eight years old, and so I can't remember very much about it. When I was about ten years old my uncle hired me out to Captain ——. I had already learned how to plow, and was also a good hand at picking cotton. I was told that the Captain wanted me for his houseboy, and that later on he was going to train me to be his coachman. To be a coachman in those days was considered a post of honor, and young as I was, I was glad of the chance.

But I had not been at the Captain's a month before I was put to work on the farm, with some twenty or thirty other Negroes —men, women and children. From the beginning the boys had the same tasks as the men and women. There was no difference.

We all worked hard during the week, and would frolic on Saturday nights and often on Sundays. And everybody was happy. The men got $3 a week and the women $2. I don't know what the children got. Every week my uncle collected my money for me, but it was very little of it that I ever saw. My uncle fed and clothed me, gave me a place to sleep, and allowed me ten or fifteen cents a week for "spending change," as he called it.

I must have been seventeen or eighteen years old before I got tired of that arrangement, and felt that I was man enough to be working for myself and handling my own wages. The other boys about my age and size were "drawing" their own pay, and they used to laugh at me and call me "Baby," because my old uncle was always on hand to "draw" my pay. Worked up by these things, I made a break for liberty. Unknown to my uncle or the Captain I went off to a neighboring plantation and hired myself out to another man. The new landlord agreed to give me forty cents a day and furnish me one meal. I thought that was doing fine. Bright and early one Monday morning I started for work, still not letting the others know anything about it. But they found it out before sundown. The Captain came over to the new place and brought some kind of officer of the law. The officer pulled out a long piece of paper from his pocket and read it to my employer. When this was done I heard my new boss say:

"I beg your pardon, Captain. I didn't know this Negro was bound out to you, or I wouldn't have hired him."

"He certainly is bound out to me," said the Captain. "He belongs to me until he is twenty-one, and I'm going to make him know his place."

So I was carried back to the Captain's. That night he made

me strip off my clothing down to my waist, ordered his fore-
man to give me thirty lashes with a buggy whip across my bare
back, and stood by until it was done. After that experience the
Captain made me stay on his place night and day—but my
uncle still continued to "draw" my money.

I was a man nearly grown before I knew how to count from
one to one hundred. I was a man nearly grown before I ever
saw a colored teacher. I never went to school a day in my life.
Today I can't write my own name, though I can read a little.
I was a man nearly grown before I ever rode on a railroad
train, and then I went on an excursion from Elberton to
Athens. What was true of me was true of hundreds of other
Negroes around me—'way off there in the country, fifteen or
twenty miles from the nearest town.

When I reached twenty-one the Captain told me I was a free
man, but he urged me to stay with him. He said he would treat
me right, and pay me as much as anybody else would. The
Captain's son and I were about the same age, and the Captain
said that, as he had owned my mother and uncle during slavery, and as his son didn't want me to leave them (since I had
been with them so long), he wanted me to stay with the old
family. And I stayed. I signed a contract—that is, I made my
mark—for one year. The Captain was to give me $3.50 a
week, and furnish me a little house on the plantation—a one-
room log cabin similar to those used by his other laborers.

During that year I married Mandy. For several years Mandy
had been the house-servant for the Captain, his wife, his son
and his three daughters, and they all seemed to think a good
deal of her. As an evidence of their regard they gave us a suit
of furniture, which cost about $25, and we set up housekeeping

in one of the Captain's two-room shanties. I thought I was the biggest man in Georgia. Mandy still kept her place in the "Big House" after our marriage. We did so well for the first year that I renewed my contract for the second year, and for the third, fourth and fifth year I did the same thing. Before the end of the fifth year the Captain had died, and his son, who had married some two or three years before, took charge of the plantation. Also, for two or three years, this son had been serving at Atlanta in some big office to which he had been elected. I think it was in the Legislature or something of that sort— anyhow, all the people called him Senator. At the end of the fifth year the Senator suggested that I sign up a contract for ten years; then, he said, we wouldn't have to fix up papers every year. I asked my wife about it; she consented; and so I made a ten-year contract.

Not long afterward the Senator had a long, low shanty built on his place. A great big chimney, with a wide, open fireplace, was built at one end of it and on each side of the house, running lengthwise, there was a row of frames or stalls just large enough to hold a single mattress. The places for these mattresses were fixed one above the other; so that there was a double row of these stalls or pens on each side. They looked for all the world like stalls for horses. Since then I have seen cabooses similarly arranged as sleeping quarters for railroad laborers.

Nobody seemed to know what the Senator was fixing for. All doubts were put aside one bright day in April when about forty able-bodied Negroes, bound in iron chains, and some of them handcuffed, were brought out to the Senator's farm in three big wagons. They were quartered in the long, low shanty, and it was afterward called the stockade. This was the beginning of the Senator's convict camp. These men were prisoners who had been leased by the Senator from the State of Georgia at about $200 each per year, the State agreeing to pay for guards and physicians, for necessary inspection, for inquests, all rewards for escaped convicts, the cost of litigation and all other incidental expenses.

When I saw these men in shackles, and the guards with their guns, I was scared nearly to death. I felt like running away, but I didn't know where to go. And if there had been any place to go to, I would have had to leave my wife and child behind. We free laborers held a meeting. We all wanted to quit. We sent a man to tell the Senator about it. Word came back that we were all under contract for ten years and that the Senator would hold us to the letter of the contract, or put us in chains and lock us up—the same as the other prisoners. It was made plain to us by some white people we talked to that in the contracts we had signed we had all agreed to be locked up in a stockade at night or at any other time that our employer saw fit; further, we learned that we could not lawfully break our contract for any reason and go and hire ourselves to somebody else without the consent of our employer; and, more than that, if we got mad and ran away, we could be run down by bloodhounds, arrested without process of law, and be returned to our employer, who, according to the contract, might beat us brutally or administer any kind of punishment that he thought proper. In other words, we had sold ourselves into slavery— and what could we do about it? The white folks had all the courts, all the guns, all the hounds, all the railroads, all the telegraph wires, all the newspapers, all the money, and nearly all the land—and we had only our ignorance, our poverty and our empty hands. We decided that the best thing to do was to shut our mouths, say nothing, and go back to work. And most of us worked side by side with those convicts during the remainder of the ten years.

But this first batch of convicts was only the beginning. Within six months another stockade was built, and twenty or thirty other convicts were brought to the plantation, among them six or eight women! The Senator had bought an additional thousand acres of land, and to his already large cotton plantation he added two great big sawmills and went into the lumber business. Within two years the Senator had in all 200 Negroes working on his plantation—about half of them free laborers, so called, and about half of them convicts. The only difference between the free laborers and the others was that the free laborers could come and go as they pleased, at night—that is, they were not locked up at night, and were not, as a general thing, whipped for slight offenses.

The troubles of the free laborers began at the close of the ten-year period. To a man they all refused to sign new contracts—even for one year, not to say anything of ten years. And just when we thought that our bondage was at an end we found that it had really just begun. Two or three years before, or about a year and a half after the Senator had started his camp, he had established a large store, which was called the commissary. All of us free laborers were compelled to buy our supplies—food, clothing, etc.—from that store. We never used any money in our dealings with the commissary, only tickets or orders, and we had a general settlement once each year, in October. In this store we were charged all sorts of high prices for goods, because every year we would come out in debt to our employer. If not that, we seldom had more than $5 or $10 coming to us—and that for a whole year's work. Well, at the close of the tenth year, when we kicked and meant to leave the Senator, he said to some of us with a smile (and I never will forget that smile—I can see it now):

"Boys, I'm sorry you're going to leave me. I hope you will do well in your new places—so well that you will be able to pay me the little balances which most of you owe me."

Word was sent out for all of us to meet him at the commissary at 2 o'clock. There he told us that, after we had signed what he called a written acknowledgement of our debts, we might go and look for new places. The storekeeper took us one by one and read to us statements of our accounts. According to the books there was no man of us who owed the Senator less than $100; some of us were put down for as much as $200. I owed $165, according to the bookkeeper. These debts were not accumulated during one year, but ran back for three and four years, so we were told—in spite of the fact that we understood that we had had a full settlement at the end of each year. But no one of us would have dared to dispute a white man's word —oh, no; not in those days. Besides, we fellows didn't care anything about the amounts—we were after getting away; and we had been told that we might too, if we signed the acknowledgment. We would have signed anything, just to get away. So we stepped up, we did, and made our marks. That same night we were rounded up by a constable and ten or twelve white men, who aided him, and we were locked up, every one of us, in one of the Senator's stockades. The next morning it was explained to us by the two guards appointed to watch us that, in the papers we had signed the day before, we had not only made acknowledgement of our indebtedness, but that we had also agreed to work for the Senator until the debts were paid by hard labor. And from that day forward we were treated just like convicts. Really we had made ourselves lifetime slaves, or peons, as the laws called us. But call it slavery, peonage, or what not, the truth is we lived in a hell on earth what time we spent in the Senator's peon camp.

I lived in that camp, as a peon, for nearly three years. My wife fared better than I did, as did the wives of some of the other Negroes, because the white men about the camp used these unfortunate creatures as their mistresses. When I was first put in the stockade my wife was still kept for a while in the "Big House," but my little boy, who was only nine years old, was given away to a Negro family across the river in South Carolina, and I never saw or heard of him after that. When I left the camp my wife had had two children by some one of the white bosses, and she was living in a fairly good shape in a little house off to herself. But the poor Negro women who were not in the class with my wife fared about as bad as the helpless Negro men. Most of the time the women who were peons or convicts were compelled to wear men's clothes. Sometimes, when I have seen them dressed like men, and plowing or hoeing or hauling logs or working at the blacksmith's trade, just the same as men, my heart would bleed and my blood would boil, but I was powerless to raise a hand. It would have meant death on the spot to have said a word. Of the first six women brought to the camp, two of them gave birth to children after they had been there more than twelve months—and the babies had white men for their fathers!

The stockades in which we slept, were, I believe, the filthiest places in the world. They were cesspools of nastiness. During the thirteen years that I was there I am willing to swear that a mattress was never moved after it had been brought there, except to turn it over once or twice a month. No sheets were used, only dark-colored blankets. Most of the men slept every night in the clothing that they had worked in all day. Some of the worst characters were made to sleep in chairs. The doors were locked and barred, each night, and tallow-candles were the only lights allowed. Really the stockades were but little more than cow sheds, horse stables, or hog pens. Strange to say, not a great number of these people died while I was there, though a great many came away maimed and bruised and, in some cases, disabled for life. As far as I can remember only about ten died during the last ten years that I was there, two of these being killed outright by the guards for trivial offenses.

It was a hard school that peon camp was, but I learned more there in a few short months by contact with those poor fellows from the outside world than ever I had known before. Most of what I learned was evil, and I now know that I should have been better off without the knowledge, but much of what I learned was helpful to me. Barring two or three severe and brutal whippings which I received, I got along very well, all things considered; but the system is damnable. A favorite way of whipping a man was to strap him down to a log, flat on his back, and spank him fifty or sixty times on his bare feet with a shingle or a huge piece of plank. When the man would get up with sore and blistered feet and an aching body, if he could not then keep up with the other men at work he would be strapped to the log again, this time face downward, and would be lashed with a buggy trace on his bare back. When a woman had to be whipped it was usually done in private, though they would be compelled to fall down across a barrel or something of the kind and receive the licks on their backsides.

The working day on a peon farm begins with sunrise and ends when the sun goes down; or, in other words, the average peon works from ten to twelve hours each day, with one hour (from 12 o'clock to 1 o'clock) for dinner. Hot or cold, sun or rain, this is the rule. As to their meals, the laborers are divided up into squads or companies, just the same as soldiers in a great military camp would be. . . . Each peon is provided with a great big tin cup, a flat tin pan and two big tin spoons. No knives or forks are ever seen, except those used by the cooks. At meal time the peons pass in single file before the cooks, and hold out their pans and cups to receive their allowances. Cow peas (red or white, which when boiled turn black), fat bacon and old-fashioned Georgia cornbread, baked in pones from one to two and three inches thick, made up the chief articles of food. Black coffee, black molasses and brown sugar are also used abundantly. . . .

Today, I am told, there are six or seven of these private camps in Georgia—that is to say, camps where most of the convicts are leased from the State of Georgia. But there are hundreds and hundreds of farms all over the State where Negroes, and in some cases poor white folks, are held in bondage on the ground that they are working out debts, or where the contracts which they have made hold them in a kind of perpetual bondage, because, under those contracts they may not quit one employer and hire out to another except by and with the knowledge and consent of the former employer.

One of the usual ways to secure laborers for a large peonage camp is for the proprietor to send out an agent to the little courts in the towns and villages, and where a man charged with some petty offense has no friends or money the agent will urge him to plead guilty, with the understanding that the agent will pay his fine, and in that way save him from the disgrace of being sent to jail or the chain-gang! For this high favor the man must sign beforehand a paper signifying his willingness to go to the farm and work out the amount of the fine imposed. When he reaches the farm he has to be fed and clothed, to be sure, and these things are charged up to his account. By the time he has worked out his first debt another is hanging over his head, and so on and so on, by a sort of endless chain, for an indefinite period, as in every case the indebtedness is arbitrarily arranged by the employer. In many cases it is very evident that the court officials are in collusion with the proprietors or agents, and that they divide the "graft" among themselves. . . .

But I didn't tell you how I got out. I didn't get out—they put me out. When I had served as a peon for nearly three years —and you remember that they claimed I owed them only $165—when I had served for nearly three years one of the bosses came to me and said that my time was up. He happened to be the one who was said to be living with my wife. He gave me a new suit of overalls, which cost about seventy-five cents, took me in a buggy and carried me across the Broad River into South Carolina, set me down and told me to "git." I didn't have a cent of money, and I wasn't feeling well, but somehow I managed to get a move on me. I begged my way to Columbia. In two or three days I ran across a man looking for la-

HELL ITSELF

borers to carry to Birmingham, and I joined his gang. I have been here in the Birmingham district since they released me, and I reckon I'll die either in a coal mine or an iron furnace. It don't make much difference which. Either is better than a Georgia peon camp. And a Georgia peon camp is hell itself!

From *The Life Stories of Undistinguished Americans As Told by Themselves,*
edited by Hamilton Holt, 1906.

146

FOUNDERS OF THE NIAGARA MOVEMENT, PHOTOGRAPHED AT THE FIRST
MEETING IN JUNE 1905. W. E. B. DUBOIS IS IN THE SECOND ROW,
SECOND FROM THE RIGHT

*B*orn *in 1868, five years after
Emancipation, W. E. B. DuBois was the great-great-grandson
of an African slave who won his freedom as a Revolutionary
soldier against the British. DuBois was schooled in his home
state of Massachusetts, and took his degrees at Fisk, Harvard*

147

—where he was the first Negro to receive the Doctorate of Philosophy—and the University of Berlin.

He launched Harvard's Historical Series in 1896 with a study of the African slave trade, and three years later published The Philadelphia Negro, *one of the earliest scientific studies of an urban minority. Teaching and writing at Atlanta University, he soon demonstrated a quality of mind that placed him in the front ranks of America's intellectuals.*

In 1903 DuBois published a book which had an enormous influence on American thinking about the Negro. Called The Souls of Black Folk, *it criticized Booker T. Washington's policy of relying on the good will of Southern whites and attacked the disfranchisement and segregation which it had failed to stop. Young as the century was, DuBois foresaw that its problem was the problem of the color-line. He urged Negro leaders to demand every right pledged in the Declaration of Independence and the Constitution.*

Two years later, in June, 1905, DuBois and about thirty other Negroes—most of them college-educated—met at Niagara Falls to announce a program based upon the principles of human brotherhood, freedom of speech and criticism, and exercise of all rights without regard to race. They would never stop protesting, they said, until America redressed its shameful treatment of the Negro.

In August, 1906, the Niagara Movement, as it was called, met again, this time at Harper's Ferry where John Brown and his Negro and white men had laid down their lives to liberate the slaves. From this meeting came a burning manifesto to the country which was written by DuBois.

No cowards or trucklers . . .

1906

THE MEN OF THE NIAGARA MOVEMENT coming from the toil of the year's hard work and pausing a moment from the earning of their daily bread turn toward the nation and again ask in the name of ten million the privilege of a hearing. In the past year the work of the Negro hater has flourished in the land. Step by step the defenders of the rights of American citizens have retreated. The work of stealing the black man's ballot has progressed and the fifty and more representatives of stolen votes still sit in the nation's capital. Discrimination in travel and public accommodation has so spread that some of our weaker brethren are actually afraid to thunder against color discrimination as such and are simply whispering for ordinary decencies.

Against this the Niagara Movement eternally protests. We will not be satisfied to take one jot or tittle less than our full manhood rights. We claim for ourselves every single right that belongs to a freeborn American, political, civil and social; and until we get these rights we will never cease to protest and assail the ears of America. The battle we wage is not for ourselves alone but for all true Americans. It is a fight for ideals, lest this, our common fatherland, false to its founding, become in truth the land of the thief and the home of the Slave—a by-word and a hissing among the nations for its sounding pretentions and pitiful accomplishment.

Never before in the modern age has a great and civilized folk threatened to adopt so cowardly a creed in the treatment of its fellow-citizens born and bred on its soil. Stripped of verbiage and subterfuge and in its naked nastiness the new American creed says: Fear to let black men even try to rise lest they become the equals of the white. And this is the land that professes to follow Jesus Christ. The blasphemy of such a course is only matched by its cowardice.

In detail our demands are clear and unequivocal.

First, we would vote; with the right to vote goes everything: Freedom, manhood, the honor of your wives, the chastity of your daughters, the right to work, and the chance to rise, and let no man listen to those who deny this.

We want full manhood suffrage, and we want it now, henceforth and forever.

Second. We want discrimination in public accommodation to cease. Separation in railway and street cars, based simply on race and color, is un-American, undemocratic, and silly. We protest against all such discrimination.

Third. We claim the right of freemen to walk, talk, and be with them that wish to be with us. No man has a right to choose another's man's friends, and to attempt to do so is an impudent interference with the most fundamental human privilege.

Fourth. We want the laws enforced against rich as well as poor; against Capitalist as well as Laborer; against white as well as black. We are not more lawless than the white race, we are more often arrested, convicted and mobbed. We want justice even for criminals and outlaws. We want the Constitution of the country enforced. We want Congress to take charge of Congressional elections. We want the Fourteenth Amendment carried out to the letter and every State disfranchised in Congress which attempts to disfranchise its rightful voters. We want the Fifteenth Amendment enforced and no State allowed to base its franchise simply on color.

The failure of the Republican Party in Congress at the session just closed to redeem its pledge of 1904 with reference to suffrage conditions at the South seems a plain, deliberate, and premeditated breach of promise, and stamps that party as guilty of obtaining votes under false pretense.

Fifth. We want our children educated. The school system in the country districts of the South is a disgrace and in few towns and cities are the Negro schools what they ought to be. We want the national government to step in and wipe out illiteracy in the South. Either the United States will destroy ignorance or ignorance will destroy the United States.

And when we call for education we mean real education. We believe in work. We ourselves are workers, but work is not necessarily education. Education is the development of power and ideal. We want our children trained as intelligent human beings should be, and we will fight for all time against any proposal to educate black boys and girls simply as servants and underlings, or simply for the use of other people. They have a right to know, to think, to aspire.

These are some of the chief things which we want. How shall we get them? By voting where we may vote, by persistent, unceasing agitation, by hammering at the truth, by sacrifice and work.

We do not believe in violence, neither in the despised violence of the raid nor the lauded violence of the soldier, nor the barbarous violence of the mob, but we do believe in John Brown, in that incarnate spirit of justice, that hatred of a lie, that willingness to sacrifice money, reputation, and life itself on the altar of right. And here on the scene of John Brown's martyrdom we reconsecrate ourselves, our honor, our property to the final emancipation of the race which John Brown died to make free.

Our enemies, triumphant for the present, are fighting the stars in their courses. Justice and humanity must prevail. We live to tell these dark brothers of ours—scattered in counsel, wavering and weak—that no bribe of money or notoriety, no promise of wealth or fame, is worth the surrender of a peoples' manhood or the loss of a man's self-respect. We refuse to surrender the leadership of this race to cowards and trucklers. We are men; we will be treated as men. On this rock we have planted our banners. We will never give up, though the trump of doom find us still fighting.

And we shall win. The past promised it, the present foretells it. Thank God for John Brown; Thank God for Garrison and Douglass! Sumner and Phillips, Nat Turner and Robert Gould Shaw, and all the hallowed dead who died for freedom!

Thank God for all those today, few though their voices be, who have not forgotten the divine brotherhood of all men, white and black, rich and poor, fortunate and unfortunate.

We appeal to the young men and women of this nation, to those whose nostrils are not yet befouled by greed and snobbery and racial narrowness: Stand up for the right; prove yourselves worthy of your heritage and whether born north or south dare to treat men as men. Cannot the nation that has absorbed ten million foreigners into its political life without catastrophe absorb ten million Negro Americans into that same political life at less cost than their unjust and illegal exclusion will involve?

Courage, brothers! The battle for humanity is not lost or losing. All across the skies sit signs of promise. The Slav is raising in his might, the yellow millions are tasting liberty, the black Africans are writhing toward the lights, and everywhere the laborer, with ballot in his hand, is voting open the gates of Opportunity and Peace. The morning breaks over blood-stained hills. We must not falter, we may not shrink. Above are the everlasting stars.

Reprinted in *An ABC of Color*, by W. E. B. DuBois, 1963.

IDA B. WELLS.

In the young twentieth century Negroes did not walk in green pastures. Many people might be living better on the strength of America's industrial machine, but not the millions born with the stigma of color.

Theodore Roosevelt's reform program was an empty promise for Negroes. As they moved from farm to city seeking jobs and decent housing they were packed into ghettoes that intensified all the ills of slum life. And almost everywhere they went, Jim Crow and the lyncher followed. In the first decade of the new century violence lurked at every corner, exploding in individual assaults or mass race riots that crazed whole cities throughout the North as well as the South.

One of the most passionate voices of protest in this period was Ida B. Wells. She was born in Mississippi four years after the end of the Civil War. At fourteen, while a student in a Freedmen's Aid Society school, she lost both parents and took over the support of four younger children. Somehow she managed to get more schooling while carrying this burden. Later she went as a teacher to Memphis and began to write for a local Negro paper, the Living War. Finally she quit the classroom to edit her own paper, Free Speech. Her courageous fight against racial injustice brought her many readers in the Mississippi Delta until 1892, when she exposed white businessmen who had instigated the lynching of three young Negro competitors. A mob wrecked her press during the night and she was forced to flee the city.

She carried her antilynch crusade to New York, writing for the Age and publishing her Red Book, the first definitive study of lynching in the United States. In 1892 she went to England to raise international support for the campaign, and the next year to Chicago where she began organizing Negro youth and women's clubs. She married the lawyer, Ferdinand Barnett, founder of the city's first Negro newspaper. At twenty-five she said, "Our work has only begun; our race—hereditary bondsmen—must strike the blow if they would be free." With her husband she worked unceasingly against the mob mania, running great risks to report social injustice on the scene and to defend its victims.

The result of one of her investigations of a double lynching is contained in this article she wrote in 1910.

Mob law in Lincoln's state . . .

1910

THE RECORD of the past ten years shows a surprising increase in lynchings and riot even in the North. No Northern state has more frequently offended in this crime than Illinois, the State of Lincoln. . . . Since 1893 there have been sixteen lynchings within the State, including the Springfield riot. With each repetition there has been increased violence, rioting and barbarism. The last lynching, which took place November 11th of last year in Cairo, was one of the most inhuman spectacles ever witnessed in this country.

The Negroes of Illinois have taken counsel together for a number of years over Illinois' increased lynching record. They elected one of their number to the State Legislature in 1904, who secured the passage of a bill which provided for the suppression of mob violence, not only by punishment of those who incited lynchings, but provided for damages against the City and County permitting lynchings. The Bill goes further and provides that if any person shall be taken from the custody of the Sheriff or his deputy and lynched, it shall be prima facie evidence of failure on the part of the Sheriff to do his duty. And upon that fact being made to appear to the Governor, he shall publish a proclamation declaring the office of Sheriff vacant, and such Sheriff shall not thereafter be eligible to either election or reappointment to the office. . . . This Bill passed both houses, was signed by Governor Deneen and became a law in 1905.

In the Springfield riot and lynching of two years later, the only parts of this law that were applicable were those providing punishment for the persons inciting rioting and lynching, and damages for the relatives of the victims of the mob. The men lynched then were not prisoners in the custody of the Sheriff, but peaceable, lawabiding citizens whom the mob lynched at their homes for the fun of it. Because of the dangerous public sentiment, which says it is all right to kill so long as the victim is a Negro, no jury has been found in Springfield to convict any of those who were tried for that lynching and murder.

On the morning of November 11th last year, a double lynching was reported from Cairo, Ill.—a white man and a Negro. A white girl had been found murdered two days before. The bloodhounds which were brought led to a Negro's house three blocks away. A Negro who had stayed in that house the night before was arrested and sweated for twenty-four hours. Although the only clew found was that the gag in the girl's mouth was of the same kind of cloth as the handkerchief of the prisoner, threats of lynching him became so frequent that the Sheriff took him away from the city, back in the woods twenty-five miles away.

When the mob had increased its numbers, they chartered a train, went after the Sheriff, brought him and his prisoner back to Cairo. A rope was thrown over Will James' neck, he was dragged off the train to the main business corner of the town. The rope was thrown over a steel arch, which had a double row of electric lights. The lights were turned on and the body hauled up in view of the assembled thousands of men, women and children. The rope broke before James was strangled to death and before hundreds of waiting bullets could be fired into his body. However, as many as could crowd around emptied their revolvers into the quivering mass of flesh as it lay on the ground. Then seizing the rope the mob dragged the corpse a mile up Washington Street, the principal thoroughfare, to where the girl's body had been found. They were followed by a jeering, hooting, laughing throng of all ages and of both sexes of white people. There they built a fire and placed this body on the flames. It was then dragged out of the fire, the head cut off and stuck on a nearby fence post. The trunk was cut open, the heart and other organs were cut out, sliced up and passed around as souvenirs of the ghastly orgy and our American civilization.

Having tasted blood, a voice in the crowd said, "Let's get Salzner." Away went the mob to the county jail. Salzner, a white man, had been indicted for wife murder and was in jail awaiting trial. The suggestion is said to have come from the brother of Salzner's murdered wife. The mob demanded that the Sheriff, who had repaired to his office in the jail when Will James had been taken from him an hour before, get Salzner for them. He begged them to go away, but when they began battering in the doors he telephoned the Governor for troops.

The lynchers got Salzner, hanged him in the court yard in front of the jail, emptied their remaining bullets in his body and went away. When troops reached the scene six hours later, they found, as the leading morning paper said next day, that "the fireworks were all over."

In mass meeting assembled the Negro citizens of Chicago called on Governor Deneen to do his duty and suspend the Sheriff. Two days later the Sheriff's office was vacated. Ten days more and Sheriff Davis had filed his petition for reinstatement, and on December 1st, argument was had before Governor Deneen both for and against the Sheriff.

The Sheriff's counsel, an ex-state Senator, and one of the leading lawyers of Southern Illinois, presented the Sheriff's petition for reinstatement, which declared he had done all in his power to protect the prisoners in his charge. He read letters and telegrams from judges, editors, lawyers, bankers, merchants, clergymen, the Mayor of the City, Captain of Company K of the State Militia, his political opponents and even the temporary incumbent of the Sheriff's office himself—all wrote to urge Sheriff Davis' reinstatement. The petitions were signed by hundreds of citizens in all walks of life and the Catholic priest of Sheriff Davis' Parish was present all day and sat at the Sheriff's side.

As representing the people who had sent me to Cairo to get the facts, I told of the lynching, of visiting the scenes thereof, of the three days' interview with the colored people of Cairo, and of reading the files of every newspaper in the city published during the lynching to find some account of the steps that had been taken to protect the prisoner. I told of the mass meeting of the Negroes of Cairo in which a resolution was

passed declaring that from Tuesday morning when Will James
was arrested, until Thursday night when he was lynched—the
Sheriff had neither sworn in deputies to aid him in defending
the prisoners, nor called on the Governor for troops. We said
that a reinstatement of the Sheriff would be an encouragement
to mobs to hang, shoot, burn and pillage whenever they felt
inclined in the future, as they had done in the past.

Governor Deneen rendered his decision a week later, re-
moving the Sheriff. After reviewing the case he said:

> "The sole question presented is, does the evidence show that
> the said Frank E. Davis, as Sheriff of Alexander County, did
> all in his power to protect the life of the prisoners and perform
> the duties required of him by existing laws for the protection of
> prisoners? . . .
>
> "Only one conclusion can be reached, and that is that the
> Sheriff failed to take the necessary precaution for the protection
> of his prisoners. Mob violence has no place in Illinois. It is de-
> nounced in every line of the Constitution and in every Statute.
> Instead of breeding respect for the law it breeds contempt. For
> the suppression of mob violence our Legislature has spoken in
> no uncertain terms. When such mob violence threatens the life
> of a prisoner in the custody of the Sheriff, the law charged the
> Sheriff, at the penalty of the forfeiture of his office, to use the
> utmost human endeavor to protect the life of his prisoner. The
> law may be severe. Whether severe or not it must be enforced.
>
> "Believing as I do that Frank E. Davis, as Sheriff of Alex-
> ander County, did not do all within his power to protect the
> lives of William James and Henry Salzner, I must deny the pe-
> tition of said Frank E. Davis for reinstatement as Sheriff of
> Alexander County, and the same is done accordingly."

Alexander County was one of the pivotal counties, politi-
cally speaking, in the last election. Sheriff Davis belonged to
the faction of the Republican party in Illinois which gave Gov-

ernor Deneen his re-election to the executive chair in 1908, by a smaller majority than four years before. It was believed that because of this the Governor was obligated to heed the wishes of Sheriff Davis' friends. But he had a higher obligation as Governor to protect the fair fame and uphold the laws of Illinois. He had the highest obligation of protecting his friends from themselves, of enforcing their respect for the majesty of the law, and of aiding them to see beyond their passions and prejudices, "so they might rise on stepping stones of their dead selves to higher things."

It is believed that this decision with its slogan "Mob law can have no place in Illinois" has given lynching its death blow in this State.

> From "How Enfranchisement Stops Lynching,"
> by Ida B. Wells-Barnett, *Original
> Rights Magazine,* June, 1910.

LANGSTON HUGHES, AGED SEVENTEEN, IN
THE UNIFORM OF HIS HIGH SCHOOL ROTC

Langston Hughes was born in 1902, in Joplin, Missouri. It was just at the time the Niagara Movement was crystallizing out of the opposition to Booker T. Washington's policies. He grew up in Lawrence, Kansas, the town that had been a battlefield in John Brown's struggle to make Kansas a free state. His grandmother, who raised him till he was twelve, was the widow of Sheridan Leary, one of John Brown's men killed in the raid on Harpers Ferry. The boy's first job was to clean the lobby and toilets of an old hotel nearby his school, for which he got fifty cents a week. Then his grandmother died, and his mother now took care of him, moving the family to Illinois and then to Ohio.

When he graduated from elementary school his classmates elected him Class Poet—although he had never written a poem—because there was no one else around to fill the post and Negroes were all supposed to have rhythm. He had to produce something for the occasion, and that was how he started to write poetry. A little later, in the Twenties, a new Negro movement developed in which dozens of young writers flowered. Most of them wrote on Negro themes, and used every literary form. The young Langston Hughes, who had moved to Harlem, became the unofficial laureate of his people and one of America's leading writers. He wrote poems, plays, short stories, novels, essays, history, biography, lyrics for opera composers, newspaper columns.

In his autobiography, Hughes tells what it was like to be a high school boy, and a Negro, in Cleveland as the First World War was beginning in Europe.

My soul is full of color . . .

1916

WE MOVED from Illinois to Cleveland. My step-father sent for us. He was working in a steel mill during the war, and making lots of money. But it was hard work, and he never looked the same afterwards. Every day he worked several hours overtime, because they paid well for overtime. But after a while, he couldn't stand the heat of the furnaces, so he got a job as caretaker of a theater building, and after that as janitor of an apartment house.

Rents were very high for colored people in Cleveland, and the Negro district was extremely crowded, because of the great migration. It was difficult to find a place to live. We always lived, during my high school years, either in an attic or a basement, and paid quite a lot for such inconvenient quarters. White people on the east side of the city were moving out of their frame houses and renting them to Negroes at double and triple the rents they could receive from others. An eight-room house with one bath would be cut up into apartments and five or six families crowded into it, each two-room kitchenette apartment renting for what the whole house had rented for before.

But Negroes were coming in in a great dark tide from the South, and they had to have some place to live. Sheds and garages and store fronts were turned into living quarters. As always, the white neighborhoods resented Negroes moving closer and closer—but when the whites did give way, they gave way at very profitable rentals. The landlords and the banks made it difficult for them to buy houses, so they had to pay the exorbitant rents required. When my step-father quit the steel mill job, my mother went out to work in service to help him meet expenses. She paid a woman to take care of my little brother while she worked as a maid.

I went to Central High School in Cleveland. We had a magazine called the *Belfry Owl*. I wrote poems for the *Belfry Owl*. We had some wise and very good teachers, Miss Roberts and Miss Weimer in English, Miss Chesnutt, who was the daughter of the famous colored writer, Charles W. Chesnutt, and Mr. Hitchcock, who taught geometry with humor, and Mr. Ozanne, who spread the whole world before us in his history classes. Also Clara Dieke, who painted beautiful pictures and who taught us a great deal about many things that are useful to know—about law and order in art and life, and about sticking to a thing until it is done.

Ethel Weimer discovered Carl Sandburg for me. Although I had read of Carl Sandburg before—in an article, I think, in the Kansas City *Star* about how bad free verse was—I didn't really know him until Miss Weimer in second-year English brought him, as well as Amy Lowell, Vachel Lindsay, and Ed-

gar Lee Masters, to us. Then I began to try to write like Carl
Sandburg.

Little Negro dialect poems like Paul Lawrence Dunbar's
and poems without rhyme like Sandburg's were the first real
poems I tried to write. I wrote about love, about the steel mills
where my step-father worked, the slums where we lived, and
the brown girls from the South, prancing up and down Central
Avenue on a spring day.

> *Just because I loves you—*
> *That's de reason why*
> *My soul is full of color*
> *Like de wings of a butterfly.*

> *Just because I loves you*
> *That's de reason why*
> *My heart's a fluttering aspen leaf*
> *When you pass by.*

I was fourteen then. And another of the poems was this
about the mills:

> *The mills*
> *That grind and grind,*
> *That grind out steel*
> *And grind away the lives*
> *Of men—*
> *In the sunset their stacks*
> *Are great black silhouettes*
> *Against the sky.*
> *In the dawn*
> *They belch red fire.*

The mills—
Grinding new steel,
Old men.

And about Carl Sandburg, my guiding star, I wrote:

Carl Sandburg's poems
Fall on the white pages of his books
Like blood-clots of song
From the wounds of humanity.
I know a lover of life sings
When Carl Sandburg sings.
I know a lover of all the living
Sings then.

Central was the high school of students of foreign-born parents—until the Negroes came. It is an old high school with many famous graduates. It used to be long ago the high school of the aristocrats, until the aristocrats moved farther out. Then poor whites and foreign-born took over the district. Then during the war, the Negroes came. Now Central is almost entirely a Negro school in the heart of Cleveland's vast Negro quarter.

When I was there, it was very nearly entirely a foreign-born school, with a few native white and colored American students mixed in. By foreign, I mean children of foreign-born parents. Although some of the students themselves had been born in Poland or Russia, Hungary or Italy. And most were Catholic or Jewish.

Although we got on very well, whenever class elections would come up, there was a distinct Jewish-Gentile division among my classmates. That was perhaps why I held many class and club offices in high school, because often when there was a religious deadlock, a Negro student would win the election. They would compromise on a Negro, feeling, I suppose, that a Negro was neither Jew nor Gentile!

I wore a sweater covered with club pins most of the time. I was on the track team, and for two seasons, my relay team won the city-wide championships. I was a lieutenant in the military training corps. Once or twice I was on the monthly honor roll for scholarship. And when we were graduated, Class of '20, I edited the Year Book.

My best pal in high school was a Polish boy named Sartur Andrzejewski. His parents lived in the steel mill district. His mother cooked wonderful cabbage in sweetened vinegar. His rosy-cheeked sisters were named Regina and Sabina. And the whole family had about them a quaint and kindly foreign air, bubbling with hospitality. They were devout Catholics, who lived well and were very jolly.

I had lots of Jewish friends, too, boys named Nathan and Sidney and Herman, and girls named Sonya and Bess and Leah. I went to my first symphony concert with a Jewish girl —for these children of foreign-born parents were more democratic than native white Americans, and less anti-Negro. They lent me *The Gadfly* and *Jean-Christophe* to read, and copies of the *Liberator* and the *Socialist Call*. They were almost all interested in more than basketball and the glee club. They took me to hear Eugene Debs. And when the Russian Revolution broke out, our school almost held a celebration.

Since it was during the war, and Americanism was being stressed, many of our students, including myself, were then called down to the principal's office and questioned about our belief in Americanism. Police went to some of the parents' homes and took all their books away. After that, the principal organized an Americanism Club in our school, and, I reckon, because of the customary split between Jews and Gentiles, I was elected president. But the club didn't last long, because we were never quite clear about what we were supposed to do. Or why. Except that none of us wanted Eugene Debs locked up. But the principal didn't seem to feel that Debs fell within the scope of our club. So the faculty let the club die.

Four years at Central High School taught me many invaluable things. From Miss Dieke, I learnt that the only way to get a thing done is to start to do it, then keep on doing it, and finally you'll finish it, even if in the beginning you think you can't do it at all. From Miss Weimer I learnt that there are ways of saying or doing things, which may not be the currently approved ways, yet that can be very true and beautiful ways, that people will come to recognize as such in due time. In 1916, the critics said Carl Sandburg was no good as a poet, and free verse was no good. Nobody says that today—yet 1916 is not a lifetime ago.

From the students I learnt that Europe was not so far away, and that when Lenin took power in Russia, something happened in the slums of Woodlawn Avenue that the teachers couldn't tell us about, and that our principal didn't want us to know. From the students I learnt, too, that lots of painful words can be flung at people that aren't nigger. Kike was one; spick, and hunky, others.

But I soon realized that the kikes and the spicks and the hunkies—scorned though they might be by the pure Americans—all had it on the niggers in one thing. Summer time came and they could get jobs quickly. For even during the war, when help was badly needed, lots of employers would not hire Negroes. A colored boy had to search and search for a job.

My first summer vacation from high school, I ran a dumb-waiter at Halle's, a big department store. The dumb-waiter carried stock from the stock room to the various departments of the store. I was continually amazed at trays of perfume that cost fifty dollars a bottle, ladies' lace collars at twenty-five, and useless little gadgets like gold cigarette lighters that were worth more than six months' rent on the house where we lived. Yet some people could afford to buy such things without a thought. And did buy them.

The second summer vacation I went to join my mother in Chicago. Dad and my mother were separated again, and she was working as cook for a lady who owned a millinery shop in the Loop, a very fashionable shop where society leaders came by appointment and hats were designed to order. I became a delivery boy for that shop. It was a terrifically hot summer, and we lived on the crowded Chicago South Side in a house next to the elevated. The thunder of the trains kept us awake at night. We could afford only one small room for my mother, my little brother, and me.

South State Street was in its glory then, a teeming Negro street with crowded theaters, restaurants, and cabarets. And excitement from noon to noon. Midnight was like day. The street was full of workers and gamblers, prostitutes and pimps, church folks and sinners. The tenements on either side were very congested. For neither love nor money could you find a decent place to live. Profiteers, thugs, and gangsters were coming into their own. The first Sunday I was in town, I went out walking alone to see what the city looked like. I wandered too far outside the Negro district, over beyond Wentworth, and was set upon and beaten by a group of white boys, who said they didn't allow niggers in that neighborhood. I came home with both eyes blacked and a swollen jaw. That was the summer before the Chicago riots.

I managed to save a little money, so I went back to high school in Cleveland, leaving my mother in Chicago. I couldn't afford to eat in a restaurant, and the only thing I knew how to cook myself in the kitchen of the house where I roomed was rice, which I boiled to a paste. Rice and hot dogs, rice and hot dogs, every night for dinner. Then I read myself to sleep.

I was reading Schopenhauer and Nietzsche, and Edna Ferber and Dreiser, and de Maupassant in French. I never will forget the thrill of first understanding the French of de Maupassant. The soft snow was falling through one of his stories in the little book we used in school, and that I had worked over so long, before I really felt the snow falling there. Then all of a sudden one night the beauty and the meaning of the words in which he made the snow fall, came to me. I think it was de Maupassant who made me really want to be a writer and write stories about Negroes, so true that people in far-away lands would read them—even after I was dead.

From *The Big Sea*, by Langston Hughes, Hill and Wang, 1940.

A CALENDAR
OF NEGRO HISTORY

1866-1916

1866 Fisk University founded. Civil Rights Act adopted. Race riots in Memphis and New Orleans. Ku Klux Klan organized. The first two Negroes ever elected to an American legislature are seated in the Massachusetts House of Representatives.

1867 Negro suffrage in District of Columbia established by Act of Congress. Reconstruction Bill adopted, dividing ten former Confederate states into five military districts and permitting their restoration into the Union upon reorganization on basis of Negro suffrage, disfranchisement of rebels, and ratification of Fourteenth Amendment. Morehouse College, Howard University, Talladega opened and Atlanta University chartered.

1868 Fourteenth Amendment adopted, defining national citizenship to include Negroes, providing federal protection to rights that might be invaded by the states, and providing proportionate reduction in representation to states denying suffrage. South Carolina holds constitutional convention and then first assembly of its new Reconstruction government, with Negroes holding majority of seats in both. Hampton Institute opened.

1869 Clark and Morgan colleges founded. Ebenezer Bassett becomes United States Minister to Haiti, probably first Negro appointed to diplomatic corps. First national Negro labor union formed at convention in Washington.

1870 4,880,009 Negroes in United States, 12.7 per cent of the population. Hiram R. Revels from Mississippi, first Negro senator, and Joseph H. Rainey of South Carolina, first Negro representative, enter Congress. Fifteenth Amendment adopted, forbidding any state from depriving citizen of his vote because of race, color, or previous condition of servitude. Colored Methodist Episcopal Church of America founded.

1871 Fisk Jubilee Singers begin first tour.

1872 First Negroes chosen as delegates to a major party convention take part in Republican convention at Philadelphia, renominating President Grant.

1874 Race riots in Louisiana and Mississippi.

1875 Civil Rights Act guarantees equal rights to Negroes in public places and prohibits their exclusion from jury duty. Blanche K. Bruce of Mississippi enters United States Senate, only Negro to serve full term there.

1877 Hayes-Tilden Compromise settles disputed presidential election by giving Presidency to the Republican candidate and withdrawing federal troops from the South. The period of "Black Reconstruction" ends with Conservatives in complete control of the South. Henry O. Flipper is first Negro to be graduated from United States Military Academy at West Point.

1879 Negro exodus from South takes place, in flight from disfranchisement and exploitation.

1880 6,580,793 Negroes in United States, 13.1 per cent of population.

1881 Frederick Douglass appointed Recorder of Deeds for District of Columbia, and Blanche K. Bruce appointed Register of Treasury by President James A. Garfield. Tuskegee Institute founded by Booker T. Washington. Tennessee enacts Jim Crow railroad car law, initiating segregation course soon followed by all Southern states. *Life and Times of Frederick Douglass* published.

1883 Supreme Court declares Civil Rights Act of 1875 unconstitutional. George W. Williams publishes the *History of the Negro Race*.

1886 Massacre of twenty Negroes at Carrollton, Mississippi.

1887 Thomas T. Fortune begins to edit the New York *Age*.

1888 *The Negro Question,* by George W. Cable, is published.

1890 7,488,676 Negroes in United States, 11.9 per cent of population. Mississippi constitution incorporates an "understanding" test for voters, restricting Negro suffrage. Many other Southern states adopt similar measures to exclude Negroes from political life.

1892 Baltimore *Afro-American* founded.

1895 Frederick Douglass dies. Booker T. Washington delivers his "Atlanta Compromise" speech.

1896 Supreme Court hands down Plessy *v.* Ferguson decision favoring Jim Crow by upholding "separate but equal" doctrine. W. E. B. Du-Bois publishes *The Suppression of the African Slave Trade* and Paul Laurence Dunbar his *Lyrics of Lowly Life*.

1898 Race riot at Wilmington, North Carolina, with eight Negroes killed. Negro units conspicuous in Spanish-American War.

1897 Alexander Crummell founds the American Negro Academy.

1900 8,833,994 Negroes in United States, 11.6 per cent of population. Chicago *Defender* founded. Washington's *Up From Slavery* appears as magazine serial. Race riot in New Orleans. National Negro Business League organized at Boston.

1901 Last post-Reconstruction Negro congressman, George H. White, ends term of office. Boston *Guardian* founded. Booker T. Washington dines at White House with President Roosevelt; South bitterly critical.

1905 Negro delegates from fourteen states, led by W. E. B. DuBois and W. Monroe Trotter, organize the Niagara Movement in meeting at Niagara Falls and call for abolition of all racial distinctions.

1906 Race riots in Atlanta, Georgia and Brownsville, Texas.

1908 Race riot at Springfield, Illinois. Jack Johnson wins heavyweight championship.

1909 National Association for the Advancement of Colored People founded. Matthew H. Henson accompanies Robert E. Peary to the North Pole.

1910 9,827,763 Negroes in United States, 10.7 per cent of population. DuBois made editor of NAACP magazine, *Crisis.*

1911 National Urban League organized.

1912 W. C. Handy's *Memphis Blues* is published.

1915 Grandfather clause, disfranchising Negroes, held unconstitutional by Supreme Court. Ku Klux Klan revived in Georgia and spreads throughout country. Southern Negroes begin migration to northern industrial centers. Association for the Study of Negro Life and History is founded by Carter G. Woodson. Booker T. Washington dies. First annual award by NAACP of Spingarn Medal made to Ernest E. Just for achievement in biology.

1916 *Journal of Negro History* begins publication. Two Negro regiments serve with General Pershing on Mexican punitive raids.

READING LIST

Aptheker, Herbert. *A Documentary History of the Negro People in the United States.* New York: Citadel, 1951.
> Several hundred documents, dating from 1661 to 1910, are included in this book of almost 1,000 pages, the most comprehensive collection available.

Bontemps, Arna, and Jack Conroy. *They Seek a City.* New York: Doubleday, 1945.
> A vivid history of Negro migration within the United States, including many biographical sketches.

Franklin, John Hope. *From Slavery to Freedom.* New York: Knopf, 1956.
> The classic, most detailed, one-volume history of American Negroes, by one of the best authorities.

Franklin, John Hope. *Reconstruction: After the Civil War.* Chicago: University of Chicago Press, 1961.
> This compact study cuts through the controversies about the Reconstruction era to give the reader a balanced picture of its course and its outcome.

Gossett, Thomas F. *Race: The History of an Idea in America.* Dallas: Southern Methodist University Press, 1965.
> Traces the development of racist ideas beginning with the settlement of America and going through Negro slavery to today's battle for civil rights against white supremacists.

Hughes, Langston, and Milton Meltzer. *A Pictorial History of the Negro in America.* New York: Crown, 1963.
> Over 1,000 prints, drawings, paintings, photos, broadsides, cartoons, posters are combined with a swift narrative in a panoramic history that comes down to the present.

Logan, Rayford W. *The Negro in American Life and Thought—The Nadir 1877-1901.* New York: Dial, 1954.
> An examination of how the political parties and the press treated the Negro in the last quarter of the nineteenth century, one of the worst periods for the American Negro.

McPherson, James M. *The Struggle for Equality.* Princeton: Princeton University Press, 1964.
> The role of the Negro and his abolitionist allies in shaping national policy during the Civil War and Reconstruction.

Meier, August. *Negro Thought in America: 1880-1915.* Ann Arbor: University of Michigan Press, 1963.
> A study of Negro thought and culture from the end of Reconstruction to World War I, the age of Booker T. Washington.

Quarles, Benjamin. *The Negro in the Making of America.* New York: Collier Books, 1964.
> A very readable survey of the Negro's past that does more than present him as a "problem"—it shows his positive contributions to American life.

READING LIST

Rose, Willie Lee. *Rehearsal for Reconstruction*. New York: Bobbs-Merrill, 1964.
A portrait in miniature of the social and political issues of Reconstruction during the experimental period on the Sea Islands of South Carolina during the Civil War.

Woodward, C. Vann. *The Strange Career of Jim Crow*. New York: Oxford University Press, 1964.
A brief but very important account of how segregation developed in the South after Reconstruction.

Index

ABOUT THE EDITOR

MILTON MELTZER has a profound interest in social reform and its effects upon all Americans. In his second volume dealing with the history of the American Negro, the author's concern is again reflected. His previous books include *A Pictorial History of the Negro in America* (with Langston Hughes), and two biographies of abolitionists—*A Light in the Dark: The Life of Samuel Gridley Howe,* and *Tongue of Flame: The Life of Lydia Maria Child.* He has written and produced a three-part film series called *Free and Equal: The History of the American Negro.*

Mr. Meltzer was born in Worcester, Massachusetts, where he went to Classical High School. He also attended Columbia University. He is the editor of a medical newspaper, and has written for magazines, newspapers, radio, television, and documentary films. He has traveled throughout the United States and Europe. Mr. Meltzer and his wife live in New York City. They have two daughters.